I Want My Marriage to Be Better

Also by Dr. Henry Brandt –

I WANT TO ENJOY MY CHILDREN

I Want My Marriage to Be Better

Dr. Henry Brandt
with
Phil Landrum

ZONDERVAN
PUBLISHING HOUSE
OF THE ZONDERVAN CORPORATION
GRAND RAPIDS, MICHIGAN 49506

I Want My Marriage to Be Better

Copyright © 1976 by The Zondervan Corporation
Grand Rapids, Michigan

Third printing   April 1977

Library of Congress Cataloging in Publication Data

Brandt, Henry R
  I want my marriage to be better.

  1. Marriage.   I. Landrum, Phil, joint author.
II. Title.
HQ734.B79   301.42   76-26480

All Scripture references are taken from the *New American Standard Bible.* Copyright 1960, 1962, 1968, 1971, 1972 by The Lockman Foundation. Used by permission.

Printed in the United States of America

To those husbands and wives
who are committed to staying with their
marriage until death

The teaming up of the authors of this book has brought together a psychologist and a journalist. Henry Brandt is the psychologist responsible for the direction and content of the book. Phil Landrum is the writer who has had years of experience in Christian journalism. *I Want My Marriage to Be Better* has come about after many hours of sifting through Dr. Brandt's notes as well as dozens of tapes and lectures. We have had long hours of discussion and revision upon revision of our efforts to capture in print the content and spirit of the lectures which have helped thousands of families find direction for Christian family living.

Our primary source of values is the Bible, which we accept as the infallible Word of God.

Henry Brandt
Phil Landrum

Contents

1 / Remember How Beautifully It All Started?

1 / Remember How Beautifully It All Started?

THE BACHELORS

There were five of them — all bachelors — working for the same organization. An impressive group. Talented. Educated (four had master's degrees). Obviously leaders of the future.

But there was something even more unusual about these five men. They vowed to each other never to get married.

We all took this vow with a grain of salt.

That was six years before, but one by one they reneged. Then the lone survivor called me.

"I'm dating a girl and we're pretty serious. It looks as if I'm going to get married, too."

Just what you would have expected.

But imagine what it cost the first member to break that bond. He had to change a relationship with four close buddies. They had helped each other professionally, enjoyed tremendous social fellowship, taken many trips together, and now. . . .

Why would a fellow want to give up something like that? Simply because *he found something better.* At least, that was his best explanation.

Fellowship with his girl friend provided something his four buddies couldn't give him.

He changed his life style without a complaint. In the past, he and his buddies would take off on well-planned bike hikes. Now, he and his girl went on little, aimless rides.

He gave up vigorous hikes with his pals to take little walks with his girl. He substituted choir practice for football games.

How do you account for that?

I LOSE A BUDDY

I can remember asking that same question. It was back when I was still running around with the guys. *And what a bunch!* There were two carloads of us dedicated to enjoying life to the hilt. A day . . . a weekend . . . a month together with this bunch was something to remember.

There was even a closer bond between my special buddy and me. We were so close we didn't even need to talk. We enjoyed simonizing a car, he on one side and I on the other. We enjoyed pitching a tent together, all without a word.

One summer, he couldn't get off work when our gang took its annual month-long fling. When we came back, he had a girl friend. Soon I was asking myself:

Why is he so different?

Everything had changed. There were three of us now, instead of two.

He still insisted that I go along on his dates. The three of us would go out somewhere, and then we would take her home first.

That changed, in just a matter of days. After that, they dropped me off first.

What was happening?

I couldn't figure it out.

Well, at least we still have our tennis matches together . . . those life-and-death dogfights on the court.

Not for long. Soon she came along and watched. Then she played, and I watched. Finally my buddy said:

"Henry, if you want to play tennis with me, get yourself a girl."

So I did, but tennis was never the same. Those

tennis matches were *sooooo slow*. I agonized through them, but not my friend. He thoroughly enjoyed them.

The trend continued. Soon he dropped out of my life completely.

We had been together almost every evening for many years. Now he had found something better.

How does the song go . . . "Those wedding bells are breaking up that old gang of mine"? It happened all around me.

MOOSE . . . IN A READING CLUB?

There was one especially rugged friend. He was strictly an outdoorsman and an athlete. He loved hunting, fishing, ball games, hiking, camping out. Moose came indoors only to devour his food.

But he sat still for Gloria. When I heard what they were doing, I could hardly believe it. They were reading a book together! Out loud! She read a chapter — and this I could hardly believe — *he read the next chapter to her*.

Moose . . . in a "reading club"?

Incredible!

He enjoyed it. She enjoyed it. They enjoyed being together. He meant to accommodate himself to her. And vice versa.

She was a music major. She liked the piano, the organ, and going to concerts. So, they went to concerts — together. Moose at a classical concert? The thought blew my mind.

GLORIA DID THAT . . . ?

There were more surprises. Gloria was at the next softball game. Naturally. Moose played on the team, and she wanted to watch him.

The next thing I knew, this chamber music girl was out in the woods with Moose, cooking over a campfire. Before this, her dish had been the finery and the elegance of a perfectly set crystal table. Now she was roasting hot dogs?

And Moose in a suit and tie? And in the fourth pew from the front in church — five minutes before the service started — so he could be there when Gloria came down from playing the organ?

Before, he was always in the back row, one of the first to duck out after the benediction.

How come?

There just comes a time when being near your boyfriend or girl friend is the most satisfying privilege in the world.

GOD MADE ME DO IT

I guess the pull is as old as mankind, for it is mentioned in an ancient book, the Bible:

> The Lord God said, "It is not good for the man to be alone; I will make him a helper suitable for him" (Gen. 2:18).

God made us, it says. Saying it reverently, He put something into us that irresistibly draws a man to a woman. Sooner or later, marriage between two people is a consuming passion. The Bible goes on to say:

> For this cause [she is suitable for him] a man shall leave his father and his mother, and shall cleave to his wife; and they shall become one flesh (Gen. 2:24).

Isn't it true that there is a real drive within all of us for one man to pair off with one woman? The people you work with . . . or play with . . . the people you socialize with don't satisfy that need.

Why not? God made us this way. We naturally team up. A man and a woman.

WELL . . . IT HAPPENED TO ME, TOO!

It happened to me, too.

And you know what? It was fun!

I found myself figuring out how many nights I could be with her — making concessions about how to dress, where to go, and with whom.

That's the way it is . . . right?

You overlook each other's faults. You push "unacceptable behavior" out of your mind. You want to be together.

She's late. You do your best not to get upset.

His shoes could be cleaner. Well, after all, what's so bad about that?

DOWN WITH CONFLICTS!

You systematically do away with anything that interferes with this relationship. You are determined not to let "little things" get in the way. You go out of your way to be nice to her parents, and she to yours.

You want to be together all the time. So much so, that sometimes it gets you in trouble with your own folks. And you'll take ridicule from your friends. Imagine the kidding Moose got:

"Hey, Moose . . . how's the reading society?"

"Hey, Moose . . . how was the concert the other night?"

You shake it off because you are having a great time. Dating is enjoyable, exhilarating. There's that anticipation of "skin-on-skin." The physical attraction is highly exciting.

I'm not saying that every boyfriend — every girl friend — is that much fun. There are the broken romances. When you're dating, if there are too many conflicts, you just drop the relationship.

But, eventually, along comes someone you like very much even when conflicts arise. So you make concessions to each other.

OFF ON THE WRONG FOOT

Granted, many marriages start on the wrong foot. In one the boy rebels against his parents. The girl admires that, for she is rebelling against her parents. So they get married on the foundation of mutual rebellion.

Another couple marries to escape an unhappy home. Maybe it was because of the romance, the physical attraction, the pleasure of petting and sexual relations — but no real interest in each other, except for mutual self-gratification.

Perhaps a pregnancy was the only reason for some others. Or another type of crisis may have clinched it. You made a stupid mistake, but your friend stood by you.

One way or another, you got together, perhaps

without much thought as to how well you were suited to each other.

HOLY WEDLOCK . . .

In my quarter century of marriage counseling and speaking all over the world on the subject of family relations, I've listened to thousands of couples tell me how they went out of their way to accommodate each other during courting days. Perhaps you were one of them. You knew, deep down, that there were irritations between you and your partner-to-be. There was unacceptable behavior, there were differences in likes and dislikes. You made concessions to each other — some easily, some reluctantly.

So you got married — more or less aware of some of the differences, but reassured that up to now you had handled them.

. . . BECOMES HOLY DEADLOCK!

The happy days of dating either continued — that is, you kept working at getting along — or faded. Differences loomed larger and were harder to ignore.

You started saying:

"She's not like she was when we were dating."

"What's happened to the man I married?"

YOUR MARRIAGE CAN BE BETTER

It's time to face facts. Whether you are rich or poor . . . educated or uneducated . . . happy or unhappy . . . healthy or sick . . . religious or irreligious . . . stunningly beautiful or average looking . . . hate each other or love each other . . . agree or disagree . . . married five days or fifty years . . . *still you are married.*

Do you want it to be better? We want to tell you how. The principles are the same for everyone.

2 / The Rude Awakening

2 / The Rude Awakening

NANCY AND KEN WERE LOVERS . . .

Everyone has at least a few good points — ability, talent, a unique kind of charm, interesting mannerisms, pleasing ways.

Put two people together, and before long irritations, conflicts, or differences of opinion arise in spite of the assets.

Nancy and Ken found this out.

Nancy was an office manager with a dozen people reporting to her. At church, she was an efficient, dependable Sunday school secretary.

With a few girl friends, she played tennis, watched the major league baseball games, and went to local basketball and football games. Work, church, and sports kept her pleasantly occupied.

But Nancy was pushing thirty.

How come I'm not married?

It was a question she asked more and more as she looked in the mirror at her pretty face and her trim, shapely figure.

Then, along came Ken.

He showed up at church, a jolly extrovert, with a friendly grin, an easy manner, a white Thunderbird, and a pocket full of money.

He liked sports, too. But at the ball park, instead of getting bleacher seats, where Nancy chose to sit, Ken got box seats. They went to the best restaurants, and he bought her nice gifts and sent flowers. Nancy battled him tenaciously on the tennis courts. She loved to listen to him chatter, and he enjoyed being listened to.

Their courtship was pleasant and happy, but there were also some questions.

She thought Ken was too extravagant with money. Maybe he talked too much — and dressed too casually. *But,* he was responsible, had a good job, and could afford to be lavish with his money.

He thought Nancy was too quiet and conservative, *but* he felt he needed someone like her.

AFTER THE WEDDING . . .

So they got married, with all the money they needed and that big, white T-bird. And they started on their honeymoon to Florida.

Although the whirlwind courtship had lasted seven months, Nancy still wasn't used to a big car or fast driving. She was used to driving at speeds around 55 to 60 miles an hour.

But in his big, powerful Thunderbird, Ken took off at 80 miles an hour the moment they got on the freeway. (This was in "pre-energy crisis" days with 70 MPH speed limits.) It was also the first time they had been on a long trip together.

The speed bothered Nancy, who nervously watched the speedometer, waiting for Ken to slow down.

Not Ken. He just barreled down the pike toward Florida.

Finally, she looked up at him sweetly as a first-day bride should, and said:

"Honey, you are going too fast."

**AN 80-MILE-AN-HOUR HUSBAND
AND A 60-MILE-AN-HOUR WIFE**

"Don't you worry your pretty little self. You'll get used to it."

Just like jolly, easygoing Ken.

He never slowed down. Imagine 60-mile-an-hour Nancy and 80-mile-an-hour Ken spending the rest of the day in that car.

There was another thing. Ken changed lanes, darted between cars, swooped around trucks. He was having a great time. But Nancy was having fits.

SECOND THOUGHTS

Come to think of it, I've always given in to Ken. Nancy gave orders all day long at work. Ken's decisiveness had been a relief. She'd enjoyed someone else making up her mind for her. But now . . .

Maybe he is just an inconsiderate person. Will it always be like this?

As the car thundered on, she recalled many times when Ken had brushed aside her comments in his jolly way.

Nancy spent the rest of the day protesting in her mind, mentally objecting to every rapid mile.

They stopped for lunch, and Nancy noticed something else about Ken. He was in a hurry to get back on the road, so he loaded his fork with food and gulped it down.

Occasionally, he would hit his tooth with the fork. She had never noticed this until now, but the more she watched, the more disgusted she became.

She sipped her iced tea properly. Across the table came a *ping!* A few minutes later, while she was cutting her steak . . . *ping!* While she was working on her vegetables . . . *ping!*

Watching him gulp his food was bad. Listening to him chomp made it worse. Add an occasional *ping*, and lunch became unbearable.

She was rattled. There was first the difference of opinion over speed . . . the style of driving . . . and now Ken was chomping and "pinging" his way through the meal. A confused Nancy trooped to the car. Ken hopped in and . . . away they went down the highway.

THE FIRST NIGHT

They came squealing up to the motel at the end of the day. Another new experience awaited Nancy — her first

21

time in a motel with a man. And after a nerve-wracking day in the big, white Thunderbird.

Ken walked into the room, unbuttoned his jacket, and let it fly. Nancy was the kind of person who always had a place for everything.

"Aren't you going to hang your jacket up?"

"What?" A look of disbelief. "Hang my jacket up?" All he'd ever done was aim his jacket at the nearest chair.

AND LATER . . .

They made it to Miami in two and a half days. Ken was hyper as they walked into the motel on the evening of their third day of marriage. He threw open the drapes and peered out at the ocean lapping at the beach in the twilight.

"Wow! What a sight! Let's get up early and watch the sun rise over the ocean."

Nancy was completely worn out from nearly three days of tension. She was also angry, critical, and unresponsive. The ocean didn't do anything for her, nor did Ken's suggestion.

And Ken? He took it in stride.

"A good night's sleep will fix you up," he said. "It's been a long trip."

At 6:00 A.M. Ken was up, kissing Nancy awake. It was the last straw for her.

"Leave me alone, Ken. I want to sleep," she told him angrily. He obliged and headed for the beach alone.

"Nothing like a brisk walk along the beach, bright and early," he said over his shoulder as he went out the door.

LEAVIN' ON A JET PLANE . . .

Nancy couldn't get back to sleep. She was wide awake and furious. Suddenly, she made up her mind, called a taxi, threw some things in a suitcase, headed for the airport, and was on her way back to Michigan.

The plane had just taken off when she realized she would have given anything to be back in that motel. She couldn't believe her actions. She had seldom been so angry and it frightened her.

On the flight back to Detroit, her thoughts flip-flopped. One moment she felt sorry and wished to rejoin jolly, impulsive Ken. The next moment found her furious over his total lack of consideration for her.

Back in Miami, Ken was startled and surprised. *After all,* he said to himself, *what did I do, but be myself?* It was a long, lonely drive back to Detroit, with many hours to think. His thoughts wandered. One moment he felt sorry for himself, the next moment he admitted his inconsiderateness.

He stopped and called Nancy a dozen times before he got back to Detroit.

In a tearful, emotional reunion they promised each other this would never happen again. But as they discussed their tragic honeymoon, they found themselves in angry shouting matches — or long silences.

So they ended up in my consulting room.

Nancy was frightened at her hostility. Yet, she became angry every time she retold the story.

Embattled Ken couldn't believe his preoccupation but still excused his actions.

WHAT WAS THE PROBLEM?

Were they mismatched? Had they deceived each other from the beginning? Was there any hope? These were their anxious questions. I tried to lessen the tension.

"This is no serious problem."

After all, Nancy was an executive who made decisions on her own all day long. She had had her own apartment and for eight years had done whatever she pleased.

The same was true with Ken. He, too, called the shots for his employees. After work he had gone his own way for years.

Two intelligent, free-thinking people — each accustomed to having other people carry out their wishes — had been thrown together. Two fine people discovered that working out a relationship involved new discoveries about each other and accommodating one another.

Ken hadn't known how upset Nancy had been. He

23

was thoroughly enjoying himself. Nancy had no idea how firm Ken could be when he made up his mind.

Are Nancy and Ken an extreme case?

Maybe. But for every Nancy who leaves a Ken, many others seriously consider it. And there are many insensitive, highly motivated Kens around.

WHAT IS THE SOLUTION?

Understand this:

First, marriage reveals your drives as no other relationship, unmasking hostility, stubbornness, and selfishness. We discuss how to face these drives in chapters 4 and 5.

Second, a good partnership dedicates time and effort to developing a mutually agreeable way of life — the subject of chapters 6 through 12.

The adjustments necessary during the honeymoon will be replaced by others again and again as life moves on.

THAT'S ANOTHER STORY!!!

I came across a few lines once that I liked very much:

> Oh, to dwell there above
> With the saints that we love.
> That will be glory!

> But to dwell here below
> With the saints that we know.
> That's another story!

To be sure, heaven is a long-range goal. In the meantime, you work at living together here below.

"I'LL SPEND MY LIFE PLEASING YOU"

Before my marriage, I intended to be the most congenial, friendly, easygoing husband ever. I thought Eva would be the most congenial, friendly, easygoing wife. One night, during our courting days, she looked up into my eyes:

"Henry, I will spend the rest of my life making you happy."

Boooooooiiiiiinnng! That rang the bell. Imagine,

someone wanting to do that! For me?

I bought that. I went even further.

"Eva, I will do the same for you." And I meant it.

You can imagine what a tender night that was. We didn't know we couldn't live up to those vows.

We went skiing on our honeymoon and got along fine. But we hit a snag the first night home.

I went to visit the boys, as always. Nothing unusual or unpredictable. These men were my lifelong friends. For years we had gone skiing together, so that night we planned a weekend skiing trip. I went home and casually informed my wife:

"I'm going skiing over the weekend with the boys."

Remember her promise? This was her first chance to make me happy. But, do you know what she said?

"No, you aren't. You're married now."

I was astonished, bewildered. I felt betrayed.

Our first big conflict. It was quite a deal. We debated for several days before I finally got my way. *No woman was going to tell me I couldn't go skiing!*

What an attitude! It hadn't taken us long to discover that our commitment to make one another happy was a flimsy one. Our first few years together were stormy years, for we were using our respective creativity and intelligence to outmaneuver each other.

Our intentions had been good, but not our ability to carry them out. We finally found an answer as Nancy and Ken did, by facing our hostility, stubbornness, and selfishness. We developed a mutually acceptable way of life, which we've modified over the years.

A TWENTY-EIGHT-YEAR FIGHT

It's unbelievable how persistently some people can fight for their own way. I think of Cecil and Frances who one day stomped angrily into my office.

He was a big man, fifty pounds overweight. She was short and equally overweight. They were twenty-eight years and four children past their honeymoon. Early in their marriage Cecil and Frances had locked horns on two issues.

She wanted him to:
1. Take her shopping every Saturday.
2. Wash the windows whenever they were dirty.

The debate continued over the years and intensified when the kids left home. Last Saturday had been the worst. As usual, she made her big, strong husband wash the windows, which he did only after a lengthy argument. Then she had criticized the job, even making him do a few windows over again.

Already fuming about the windows, Cecil reluctantly went shopping with her. Can you picture this husky, gruff 250-pound man pushing a cart and glowering behind his aggressive 200-pound wife? All he could think of was her criticism of his window-washing job — and the football game he was missing.

When they got home, he sprang from the car and raced for the house to tune in the game. But she was right behind him.

"Oh, no, you don't get out of it that easily. You're going to help me bring these groceries in." Can you imagine two people in their fifties acting like this?

Cecil gave in again, but grumbled as he carried two of the grocery bags into the house. He deposited them and headed toward the TV. Frances had a different idea.

"Wait a minute. There's still another bag in the car."

It was the last straw. Cecil grabbed her shoulders and shook her until her teeth rattled. This near-violent attack frightened both of them. So, they were in my consulting room.

NOT FACING UP

What's their problem? Imagine fighting for twenty-eight years over washing windows and shopping! That's dedication — but the wrong kind.

To continue their marriage, Cecil and Frances must face the same basic issues which confronted Ken, Nancy, Eva, and me — hostility, stubbornness, selfishness. Then they must develop a mutually agreeable way of life.

THE RUDE AWAKENING

TEN COUPLES IN TROUBLE

My phone rang recently as I was walking out the front door. The call was from out west.

"Dr. Brandt, there are ten couples out here who are about ready to break up their marriages.

"Mine is one of the ten," the lady continued. "None of us wants to break up. Could you come out and help us turn our marriages around?"

Ten couples! Asking for help.

Many people need help these days. Every year the divorce statistics climb. In 1975 there were more than a million divorces for the first time in American history. Then there is the other side — the ten couples who want to make their marriages go.

Surely these two million persons who got divorces didn't get married with the idea of fighting each other, hating the sight of each other.

On July 3, 1975, the headline on Ann Landers' column read: "Ann Has No Answer." In the column, she wrote:

> The sad incredible fact is that after 36 years of marriage, Jules and I are being divorced. As I write these words, it is as if I am referring to a letter from a reader. It seems unreal that I'm writing about my own marriage . . .
>
> That we are going our separate ways is one of life's ironies. How did it happen that something so good for so long didn't last forever? The lady with all the answers does not know the answer to this one.
>
> Perhaps there is a lesson there for all of us. At least, it is for me. Never say, "It couldn't happen to us."

What sobering, chilling news.

THERE IS HOPE

Yes, it could happen to anyone.

Is there an answer? We think there is. It involves understanding how walls that lead to divorce are built . . . and understanding how to dismantle them and restore the pleasant, happy days of comfortable fellowship.

3 / The Walls Go Up . . . and the Marriage Comes Tumbling Down!

3 / The Walls Go Up . . . and the Marriage Comes Tumbling Down!

WHAT WE DIDN'T KNOW

Nancy and Ken believed marriage would eliminate misunderstandings, loneliness, and emptiness. They received a rude awakening on their honeymoon.

My wife and I were jolted the day we came home from our honeymoon. We figured marriage would banish conflicts. No more problems with parents or brothers or sisters. We would do as we pleased and express ourselves freely. To our dismay, we clashed on a simple decision.

"DOCTOR, HOW IS IT POSSIBLE THAT . . . ?"

I have talked with thousands of couples, young and old alike, whose hopes for a happy marriage have been dashed. We discuss the same questions:

How is it possible . . . to feel so harshly toward someone you once felt such tenderness for?

How is it possible . . . to be repulsed at the idea of being touched by a person whom you once so desired that restraint was the constant problem?

How is it possible . . . to have such sharp, unsolved conflicts when you once got along so well?

A MATTER OF WALLS . . .

How? Why? It's a matter of walls. Invisible walls

loom up and cut off affection, tenderness, and the will to work at your relationship as you did during dating days.

It even happens in those "perfect" marriages. Consider Susan and Eric. They had everything — housing, financial security, education, good background.

All set, right?

Well, in just a few months, they were in my consulting room puzzling over the coldness that had wedged them apart.

She couldn't respond to his caresses, which was no problem the first few months of their marriage. So, why now?

A wall had gone up . . . and a marriage was slowly coming down. Watch as Susan and Eric build this wall, one incident at a time, as a brick wall is built one brick at a time.

SUSAN AND ERIC . . . THEY DID THINGS RIGHT

It all started before marriage.

You couldn't find two more efficient people than Susan and Eric. He was a college graduate — handsome, talented, neat. She had her bachelor's degree and was an excellent executive secretary. In addition, she was pleasant — and beautiful.

Between them, they had saved enough money to buy a home. So they spent their engagement looking for a building site, working on plans with an architect, and then actually building the house.

This marriage was for keeps.

When the house was built and furnished, the lawn in, the driveway down, they were ready to get married. And they did. Some fantastic start for a marriage, right?

Oh, there had been some debates over the building site and house plans — even over the furniture.

But it was *so much fun* to make up after a quarrel. Flashes of anger were soothed with a gentle hug, a verbal tirade calmed with a tender kiss. Differences of opinion were carefully aired and settled. So it seemed.

Vaguely, Susan sensed the settlements usually ended up Eric's way. *But then, he did have such a logical mind. And my reasoning, well, sometimes it's not so good.*

Still, I like some of those ideas even if I can't defend them.

So she went along with Eric's reasoning and filed her ideas away.

To Eric, Susan seemed a bit illogical at times, but she caught on quickly. So he brushed aside a wispy irritability over her resistance to his ideas.

THE WALL STARTS BUILDING

Along here the wall begins. Only some of the issues were settled, only some of the anger appeared on the surface.

Susan opposed three changes in the house plans but, in the interests of peace (so she said), she let them pass.

A number of Susan's ideas irritated Eric. *They were so silly.* But, in order to build a solid relationship (?), he suppressed his reactions and smiled.

That's how they started their marriage. It was the same old thing . . . hidden irritability . . . stubbornness . . . selfishness . . . that sequence that dooms so many marriages.

They didn't realize that a thought tucked away and unspoken, an irritable spirit suppressed, a critical attitude ignored . . . build an invisible wall that slowly divides a couple. It cuts off the affection between them and cements in place tensions and thoughts unknown to each other.

Up to now, Eric and Susan had kept their true feelings and thoughts to themselves.

But maybe it wouldn't matter. Their situation was a dream come true. Even with these initial problems, it still had to be a super marriage.

THE GREAT COBWEB INCIDENT

But it all came apart.

All because of a little cobweb. Or so it seemed.

The drama began one evening a few months after their beautiful wedding ceremony. Eric came home and — he couldn't believe it! Of all things! There in the corner of the living room ceiling of his nice home was . . . a cobweb.

Hmm. She hasn't noticed it, yet. I'll not say anything to her. She'll probably get it tomorrow.

So he didn't mention it.

He did the standard things a young man should do when he comes home from work. He took Susan in his arms, kissed her, and told her how much he loved her.

The next evening, the cobweb was still there.

Again, Eric took Susan in his arms, kissed her, and said:

"I love you — very much!"

And also the third evening. By the fourth evening — even though he was still hugging, kissing, and whispering sweet words — Eric was mad.

There's that cobweb, doggone it.

Doesn't she see it?

By the fifth evening, he was kissing her with his eye on the cobweb. And by the seventh, he was so disgusted he could hardly contain himself.

AND ON THE SEVENTH DAY, HE . . .

For six days Eric had added to the invisible wall, which was made from the following:

1. Keeping his thoughts to himself.
2. Deceiving his wife . . . pretending all was well.
3. Concealing his hostility.

For those six evenings he had kissed her, hugged her, and said the same words. Now it was the seventh evening, and the words were spilling out once again.

"Susan, you're wonderful. I really love you. I'm glad I married . . . "

This time he broke off in mid-sentence. He couldn't go on with the act any more. He'd finally gotten enough nerve.

"Susan," he said sweetly, though tentatively. "Do you see that cobweb? Do you know how long it's been up there? This is the seventh day."

Susan stepped back from the embrace, looked up, and discovered the cobweb.

Now what do you think she said?

What would you have said?

Well, beautiful little Susan put her arms around Eric and answered:

"Eric. I am so glad I am married to you. You help

me be a better woman." Then she kissed him and went to the kitchen to get a broom.

Eric felt like a heel.

Look how mad I was and how nicely she took it. I ought to be ashamed of myself.

But he didn't know Susan wasn't taking it well. All the way to the kitchen she was thinking:

Good grief, if it bothered him that much, why didn't he clean it up himself? Maybe that thought occurred to you, too.

But when she came back to the scene of the cobweb with the broom, her manner was pleasant and she sweetly whisked the cobweb away.

Eric felt guilty.

What a sweet kid she is. I shouldn't have made such a fuss. But maybe I did help her. We don't want any cobwebs in the living room.

THE EFFICIENCY EXPERT GOES TO WORK!

There were several weeks of peace around the house. Silence would be a better word, for Susan was doing a slow burn over the Great Cobweb Incident. But she didn't act like it. Her manner toward Eric was beautiful. She had inadvertently spent two weeks adding to the wall between them. Her contribution?

1. Deception . . . pretending appreciation.
2. Resentment.

Then, one day, another incident. This time, it was about the dishes . . . or rather the way Susan was doing the dishes.

She was working away, putting the dishes on a drainer (they had decided against getting an electric dishwasher). And Eric, a professional efficiency expert, noticed something wrong.

She was washing dishes cross-handed! In other words, she washed dishes with her right hand then deposited them in the dish drainer to her left.

"Honey," he said, "do you realize you are washing dishes cross-handed?" Then to lessen the sting:

"Just a little tip to help you" — followed by a

nervous laugh. However, his uncertainty became scorn when Susan answered quizzically:

"Cross-handed? What's that?"

He couldn't believe it! His wife didn't know what cross-handed was. So he showed her the "most efficient way to do dishes," explaining *impatiently* how it would be easier to put the dish drainer to her right.

Do you know what Susan said?

What would you have said?

Well, she wiped her hands on her apron, put her arms around her husband, and kissed him.

"Eric, I appreciate that. I'd never have thought of it myself." Then she turned back to her dishes, doing them Eric's way.

Again, Eric felt terrible. He had been so disgusted, and she had been so nice. But he thought:

I think I did right. I really helped her.

But that's not what Susan was thinking as she turned back to the dishes.

Oh, brother! she griped to the dishwater, *is he going to tell me how to run my kitchen, too?*

She stifled her protests and kept smiling, hugging, and kissing. Eric was encouraged and increased his "suggestions." After all, shouldn't you believe your wife's (or husband's) words?

Over some weeks he had rearranged the cupboard, pantry, and other parts of the kitchen "more efficiently." Each time, Susan responded, as on cue:

"Oh, thank you, Eric."

But her resentment grew with every comment.

WORKING TOGETHER . . . AT WHAT?

This contest went on for several months, with both Susan and Eric hard at work building their wall.

His contribution:	Her contribution:
1. Deception . . . not sharing his thoughts.	1. Deception . . . pretending appreciation.

2. Impatience . . .
toward her
work habits.

2. Resentment . . . of
his interference.

3. Disgust . . . with
her "stupidity."

3. Rebellion . . .
carrying out the
changes reluctantly.

ERIC MEETS A SUDDEN WATERLOO

Then came the crisis, the big battle.

You guessed it . . . another cobweb.

In the same living room, same corner. And he waited the same seven days, then repeated the earlier scene.

"Susan, do you know how long that cobweb has been there?" he asked, expecting a loving kiss, hug, and a thank you.

No way. Fire replaced love in Susan's eyes. Her body bristled, and she stormed in all her fury:

"I'm getting sick and tired of your suggestions! Why don't you mind your own business?"

Woweeeee!

Boy, was he surprised!

We aren't, are we? We could see it coming all along. But not Eric. He had taken her at her word. He wasn't a mind reader. No one is.

Eric recoiled — at his defensive best.

"O.K., O.K.," he said. "I shouldn't have bothered you about it anyway. You've got every right to be mad."

It was a lie. This time he was pretending.

If that's the way you're going to act, I'm certainly not going to help you any more.

Now, both Susan and Eric were keeping their thoughts to themselves. And it got worse — so bad that I heard the story in my consulting room.

"We don't fight, Dr. Brandt," she told me.

"But there's tension. When his car pulls into the driveway, I find myself freezing up. I want to give him a warm welcome, but when he walks into the house, and I see his eyeballs sweep the ceiling, it turns me cold."

Their hugs were just so much bodily movement now. Their kisses were nothing more than a damp experience. Like the old song:

There's a wall between us.
It's not made of stone.
The more we are together . . .
The more we are alone.

THE CAUSE OF MOST SEX PROBLEMS

Like countless other couples, Susan and Eric were puzzled over their "sex problem." And they definitely had one.

Susan froze up at the sight of Eric. Was he less manly now? Had she lost her normal desires? Not at all. They were both very much alive. She was as pretty, witty, and sensuous as ever. He was as handsome, stable, and virile as ever.

They were divided by an invisible wall as real as if it were made of bricks. It was made out of familiar materials:

deception	rebellion
hatred	self-centeredness
resentment	impatience

WHAT HAPPENED?

Did the marriage create these reactions in Susan and Eric?

No. Marriage revealed them.

But these people were educated, responsible, well housed, well clothed, and well fed.

Yes. These benefits are highly desirable, but they don't provide what you need to handle deception, hatred, resentment, rebellion, self-centeredness, or impatience.

Eric and Susan tried to handle these reactions by holding them in. Nancy and Ken just let them come out. Both couples ended up in the consulting room. We tackle the solution in chapter 4. We comment on sex problems in chapter 11.

BIG WALLS COME FROM LITTLE BRICKS

Incredible, isn't it, that people get so distressed over driving, neatness, eating habits, time, housekeeping?

But we do. One incident doesn't mean that much, but the daily grind takes its toll. Picking up a towel that was thrown carelessly at the tub isn't so bad once. Even four times a day (twenty-eight times a week) can be tolerated.

But four times a day for six months? After a while, you start resenting it.

THEY'RE ALL AROUND THE HOUSE . . .

Think of the little issues that can pile up around the house. *Start with the living room.*

* What do you do with the newspaper? Fold it neatly on the coffee table? Or leave it strewn around the room, a section here, a section there?

* When you come home from work, do you change clothes before you sit down in the living room? Or lounge around with your grubby clothes on?

Let's move into the bedroom.

* How cool do you set the air conditioner? How high do you open the window?

* How many blankets do you sleep under?

* Do you undress with the blinds down and the lights on? Or leave the blinds up and undress in the dark?

Take the bathroom:

* What do you do with wet towels? Drape them over the shower curtain? Over the bathtub? Put them in the clothes hamper? Or hang them neatly on the rack?

* Do you install the toilet paper with the paper coming down from the top or up from the bottom of the roll?

* Where do you put the toothbrushes?

* Do you start on a new tube of toothpaste before you've squeezed the old tube flat? How do you squeeze the tube?

Move into the dining room:

* Do you keep the different foods separated on your plate or mix them together?

* How do you serve the mustard and catsup? In bottles . . . or in pretty little dishes?

* How do you cut the meat? Slice off a bite, eat it, then slice off another bite? Or cut the entire piece into many small bites first and then eat it?

* What about breakfast cereal? Pour the milk on first . . . or sprinkle the sugar first?

* How do you appear for breakfast? All dressed? Or in your bathrobe?

One disagreement doesn't amount to much. Enough of them over a period of months build an invisible, divisive wall.

We can compare it to constructing a building. One brick is hardly noticeable. Enough bricks make an enclosure that keeps you out.

In the consulting room, I hear many puzzled partners say:

"We're just not close any more."

"I can't stand him even touching me."

"There's nothing of value between us."

These are statements made by people who once thought marriage to *that same person* was a great idea.

REACTIONS TO OPINIONS ARE THE KEY

The clashes we've discussed involved differences of opinions between marriage partners. Their *reactions* to these clashes erected invisible walls that short-circuited the tenderness, fellowship, and will to make the partnership grow. It happens to newlyweds, old-timers, the educated, the wealthy, the healthy, the uneducated, the sick, and the poor.

Now, let's dismantle those walls.

4 / A Change of Heart

4 / A Change of Heart

"MY MARRIAGE IS RIDDLED WITH LOVE, HARMONY, HAPPINESS, CONSIDERATION . . ."

In twenty-five years of counseling, I've never had a couple come to see me because their marriage was riddled and torn apart with harmony, happiness, good will, consideration for one another, joy, and peace.

Can you imagine Susan and Eric coming to the consulting room beaming at each other with admiration, affection, and approval?

"We have a serious problem," Susan says. "I'm just thrilled when Eric's car pulls into the driveway. Both of us are ecstatic every time we touch each other.

"Eric approves of my every move, agrees with all my opinions, and acts on all my wishes immediately and wholeheartedly."

"Dr. Brandt, please tell us how to start a fight. We can't stand all this harmony and good will."

NO WAY . . . IT'S DISAGREEMENT AND DISCORD

No way. Each case in the last two chapters contained the common thread of *disagreement*. Let's recall a few instances:

    * How fast do you drive?
    * What about eating habits?

* What about going skiing?
* What about housekeeping techniques?

None of these are serious problems, but they illustrate two facts:

1. Disagreement is as natural as breathing when any decision is called for and opinions differ.
2. Disagreement reveals hostility, stubbornness, rebellion, and self-seeking.

Why does this happen to good, responsible people?

"YOU'VE GOT TO BE KIDDING!"

One explanation has stood the test of time. It is found in the Bible.

"Now you must be kidding!" is the first reaction from many clients.

Yet, I've seen thousands reconsider their first negative reaction to the Bible. After a few years of studying and putting its principles into practice, they found how to become wholesome individuals and have healed their marriages.

O.K. You're interested. Briefly, here's how the Bible explains the behavior of the people we discussed in chapters 2 and 3.

THE CAUSE

Let's start with the basis for good human relations. Read these verses carefully.

> Make my joy complete by being of the same mind, maintaining the same love, united in spirit, intent on one purpose. Do nothing from selfishness or empty conceit, but with humility of mind let each of you regard one another as more important than himself; do not merely look out for your own personal interests, but also for the interests of others (Phil. 2:2-4).

All of them — Ken and Nancy, Henry and Eva, Susan and Eric — agreed with these verses. They felt they wanted a loving, agreeable, unselfish relationship with one another. Yet, they all missed it.

Why?

Here comes the reason, according to the Bible:

> All of us like sheep have gone astray, each of us has turned to his own way; but the LORD has caused the iniquity of us all to fall on Him (Isa. 53:6).

There it is. When a decision was necessary, however small, and opinions differed, each of our characters turned to his own way, rather than looking out for the best interests of the partnership.

Their "iniquity" was wanting their own way, and can be summed up in one word: self-seeking. Marriage magnifies, rather than eliminates, self-seeking.

Our characters also became contentious and angry. The Bible puts it like this:

> The *deeds of the flesh* are evident, which are; immorality, impurity, sensuality, idolatry, sorcery, enmities, strife, jealousy, outbursts of anger, disputes, dissensions, factions, envyings, drunkenness, carousings and things like these, of which I forewarn you . . . that those who practice such things shall not inherit the kingdom of God (Gal. 5:19-21).

In each of our cases, marriage magnified, rather than eliminated, these "deeds of the flesh." It's normal to pursue your own way. When your path clashes with another person, automatic disagreement and "deeds of the flesh" are the result. You expected marriage to make you loving, kind, and unselfish. But it didn't.

It brought out characteristics you never liked. So where do you turn for help?

THE CURE

Godward. Does that sound too simple? Are these Bible verses heavy reading for you? Well, read on, for they hold the key to a successful marriage. Look once more at Isaiah 53:6:

> All of us like sheep have gone astray, each of us has turned to his own way; but the LORD has caused the iniquity of us all to fall on Him.

"Him" refers to Jesus. The whole chapter (Isa. 53) predicts how Jesus would die for our iniquities:

> He was pierced through for our transgressions, He was crushed for our iniquities; the chastening for our well-being

fell upon Him, and by His scourging we are healed (Isa. 53:5).

You need to be saved from your iniquities. But how? The Bible says:

> Your iniquities [self-seeking] have made a separation between you and your God, and your sins (deeds of the flesh) have hid His face from you, so that He does not hear (Isa. 59:2).

This separation can be healed easily. It is Jesus who said:

> I am the way, and the truth, and the life; no one comes to the Father, but through Me (John 14:6).

This is what the Bible says about Jesus:

> If you confess with your mouth Jesus as Lord, and believe in your heart that God raised Him from the dead, you shall be saved; for with the heart man believes, resulting in righteousness, and with the mouth he confesses, resulting in salvation (Rom. 10:9,10).

> But as many as received Him [Jesus], to them He gave the right to become children of God, even to those who believe in His name (John 1:12).

You bridge the separation between God and you by asking Jesus to come into your life. This simple step may be familiar to many readers. But for some this is new.

How can it be said more clearly? Without taking this step, there is no way to heal the drives that build walls between you and your partner.

If you've never done so, you can ask Jesus to come into your life through a simple prayer as follows:

> Jesus, I am separated from God because of my iniquities and sins. I do receive You into my life, so I can be saved from my sins and become a child of God. Thank You, Jesus, for coming into my life and bridging the separation between God and me.

If the Bible is true and you prayed sincerely, then you are now a child of God and can claim some resources that only God can make available.

46

BACK TO YOUR MARRIAGE

Remember? We are searching for a way to make your marriage better. You still fight with your partner. You do clash, turn to your own way and respond with deeds of the flesh when opinions differ. Whether you have just now become a child of God, or have been one for years, your problem has not gone away. The Bible says:

> If we confess our sins, He is faithful and righteous to forgive us our sins and to cleanse us from all unrighteousness (1 John 1:9).

I have watched many men and women choke on admitting that "I am a self-seeking person. My own way is more important to me than the best interests of my marriage. I cannot stop it without help."

You struggle with such a glimpse of yourself. But it's true, and a prayer for help is the first order of business. Your prayer can be very simple:

> God, I confess to self-seeking and deeds of the flesh when decisions come up between my partner and me. Forgive me and cleanse me. Amen.

Did you pray that prayer in sincerity? Then you are now forgiven, clean, and righteous. Now you can start over again to make your marriage better.

5 / Love Is More Than a Tingle

5 / Love Is More Than a Tingle

THE ADVANTAGE IS YOURS

So you're a child of God. Let's review what has happened to you. The Bible says:

> Therefore having been justified by faith, we have peace with God through our Lord Jesus Christ (Rom. 5:1).

Justified? What does justified mean? Here's what you, a justified person, have done:

1. Recognized the fact that your iniquities (self-seeking and deeds of the flesh) have separated you from God (Isa. 59:2).

2. Believed by faith that God has placed your iniquities on Jesus (2 Cor. 5:21; Gal. 3:13).

3. By inviting Jesus to come into your life you have been forgiven. You're a child of God and can walk into His presence (as though you never sinned), talk to Him, and *expect Him to help you* (John 1:12).

A NEW RESOURCE

How can God's resources help you? Here is the good news:

> . . . the love of God has been poured out within our hearts through the Holy Spirit who was given to us (Rom. 5:5).

The love which produces harmonious living *is not*

generated between people. It comes from outside yourself and starts with God's love. Whether you received Christ long ago or just today, you have access to His love. Ask Him to bathe your heart with it. You will be amazed at the change in your reactions to your partner. But you need to know what you are asking for.

THE OIL THAT ELIMINATES FRICTION . . . GOD'S LOVE

If you would take a sample of crude oil and break it down into its elements, you would get a variety of products including:

kerosene	ethane
gasoline	propane
methane	butane
grease	lubricating oils

Likewise, the love of God can be broken into its elements. The Bible does this in 1 Corinthians 13:4-8.

In that Scripture passage, it says:

*Love is patient	*Love does not rejoice in unrighteousness
*Love is kind	*Love does rejoice in the truth
*Love is not jealous	*Love bears all things
*Love is not arrogant	*Love believes all things
*Love does not seek its own	*Love hopes all things
*Love is not provoked	*Love endures all things
*Love does not take into account a wrong suffered	*Love never fails

Some kind of list, isn't it? Since drawing upon the love of God is so important, let's take a long look at it, so you can know how He can help.

LOVE IS PATIENT (LONG-SUFFERING)

We all get into situations we don't like. We assume the only kind of suffering is our kind.

A few years ago I was in a foreign country. If you

went anywhere you either walked or rode a donkey. All around me people were starving. It was a pitiful sight. Little children with distended stomachs stared listlessly into space, their parents helpless.

So I was relieved to get back to Miami. I was met at the airport and whisked away in a convertible over incredibly smooth highways. We went to a cafeteria which featured every kind of salad, vegetable, meat, and dessert. Yet many there were impatient, grumbling, and complaining because they had to wait in line. The wait frustrated their plans and revealed a lack of the love of God (patience).

My mind flashed back to that foreign country. Over there I found both patient and impatient people, just as in this cafeteria line.

Many people face poverty, lack of food, shabby clothes, evictions. Others never miss a meal but react impatiently.

It is not a question of poverty or plenty. It is the love of God in you that determines whether you will respond patiently or impatiently.

Some people can't find anyone to marry and are miserable. Yet, in my consulting room, I talk to people who suffer because they did find someone to marry.

"I've had enough. I can't stand any more!" as though my client is the only one who has trouble with a partner.

Everyone does.

Impatience is a common malady. Circumstances and the people in your life reveal it. What is the answer? You can shake your fist in God's face as if to say:

"God, I don't like the way You play the game!"

Or you can let God bathe your heart with love that exudes patience. Your problem doesn't go away, but you can think straight and quietly seek a solution which may take weeks, months, or even years. Your response changes in the face of suffering and problems. That's important, for you don't determine the hardships of your life or how long you suffer. Some people suffer all their lives.

Love is patient — even while a person is suffering. Patience is especially needed when dealing with children.

One couple was driven into my consulting room by their impatience.

"If we've told our son once, we've told him a hundred times to clean up his room. He's driving us up a wall. Patience doesn't work. When we run out of patience, we make him do it. Impatience is what works."

My answer?

"Your son's choices reveal your impatience, not your patience. You impatiently allowed him to keep a messy room, and then you impatiently made him clean it up. You think inaction is evidence of patience, and action is evidence of impatience. Not so. You lack patience whether you make him do it or allow him not to do it. You're confusing patience with supervision. Any businessman knows that he must provide daily supervision to assure that his employees do what is required. The old rule of thumb is: the employee will do what the boss inspects, not what he expects.

"If adults need daily supervision, how much more do children need it. All of us tend to go our own way, including children.

"The patience you need while you supervise your child is available to you from God.

"How do you get it? You admit you don't have it, repent, and ask God to bathe your heart with patience as you work *with your son* to get his room cleaned up."

Love is patient.

LOVE IS KIND

Kindness is connected to patience, extending kindness in the direction of the source of suffering. Kindness was missing in that white Thunderbird. Kindness was missing in Eric and Susan's new home. They clashed over what was best for each other.

They were dedicated to one another, but their impatience and unkindness built a wall.

I listened to a story that will benefit all of us. The speaker was a highly·educated, well-respected man, married twenty years.

His wife had a firm, unshakable conviction that it

was the duty and responsibility of the man of the house to take out the garbage. So, every morning after he kissed her good-by, she would hand him a bag or two of garbage. His normal routine was to grab the bags, stomp out of the house, and slam the garbage into the can.

"That takes care of your old garbage," he would mutter to no one, get into his car, and send it squealing around the corner.

A twenty-year battle.

Then he discovered the love of God. It startled him to realize what an unkind act he was performing every morning.

He still carries out the garbage. It's still a concession, but it is done now with a kindly spirit toward his wife.

He discovered further that he carried out many of his other daily duties with the same unkindly spirit. He realized he was the architect of his own misery.

This man let the love of God bathe his miserable spirit. Without changing a single detail in his life, he began enjoying the jobs instead of seeing them as distasteful chores.

A corporation I worked for was civic minded and pressured its employees to give a day's pay to the annual United Fund drive. There was much griping and complaining, but most employees fell in step. Some made a contribution with a kindly spirit, some under much protest. In either case, you wrote a check. It's the spirit, not the deed, that demonstrates kindness.

We are all called upon to do things we would rather not do. To do them with an unkindly spirit is to create our own suffering.

Love is kind.

LOVE IS NOT JEALOUS

Jealousy can result in terrible personal suffering. I refer to discontent, ill will, resentment, spite, unhappiness, mental uneasiness toward someone's success, superiority, or advantage. It could involve animosity toward a rival or suspected infidelity. This condition comes up frequently in the consulting room.

Jean and Martha were college pals. Jean fell for the school's star athlete and married him, only to discover he was an average person, apart from his athletic ability.

Now, Jean and her husband live in a tiny house and barely make ends meet on her husband's low salary. He happily spends evenings playing on neighborhood teams. The spectators love him.

Martha married a bookworm. Jean couldn't stand him, but the bookworm ended up doing well in the business world. Martha lives in a big, beautiful home, wears elegant clothes, drives a big car, and moves in professional circles.

Jean burns with jealousy over her husband's popularity and Martha's comfortable life. This is the opposite of admiration and happiness toward a person.

Malcolm has a knack for making profitable land deals which his wife, Helen, cannot understand. If he followed her advice he would never get involved, because she is sure he is making a mistake. His judgment bothers her, even though she benefits. This is another type of jealousy.

The love of God is the opposite of jealousy. His love would help Jean and Helen to appreciate the talent, ability, and opportunities of other people.

Love is not jealous.

LOVE DOES NOT BRAG . . .
IS NOT ARROGANT . . .

Carl came to see me for two reasons. His wife disliked him, and he was having trouble keeping friends.

After that introduction, he went ahead and chronicled his success in the insurance business. Then he told me about his college athletic career, where his name was a household word and autograph-seekers made him the center of attention.

At this moment, Carl's wife cut in.

"I've heard that same speech hundreds of times." I soon realized that Carl's conversations were one-sided. He didn't listen to other people, just waited for them to pause so he could resume bragging.

According to his wife, his business success was just average among their friends, who could care less about his college career. To them, he was just an arrogant person.

She was right. Carl demanded consideration not due him and was self-assertive beyond the bounds of modesty. That's bragging and arrogance.

THEN, THERE'S DON . . .

I was a speaker recently at a family camp. We had a leader named Don who had the ability to set a group of strangers at ease quickly. He remembered names. Before you knew it, you were singing lustily and getting acquainted. He used his talents to bless others instead of to impress — the opposite of bragging and arrogance.

The love of God does not brag. It is not arrogant.

LOVE DOES NOT ACT UNBECOMING
LOVE DOES NOT SEEK ITS OWN
LOVE IS NOT EASILY PROVOKED

These three characteristics of love can be combined: love does not act unbecoming because it does not seek its own and, therefore, is not provoked.

Sometimes, however, there are surprises in store for you. To your amazement, you are saying and doing things that hardly fit these three elements of the love of God.

As a speaker, I am often away from home. When our children were small, we had an ironclad rule: I would never be away for a full week.

Once, when 2,000 miles away from home, two days of my tour were cancelled. My next commitment was 500 miles away. What to do? Stick around or go home?

I'll do it. I'll go home and surprise them.

So I did. Two thousand miles. And after flying all night long, I arrived home about 8:30 A.M.

My wife was just leaving. It was a letdown, but, after all, she had her plans. And I hadn't called her. My arrival was to be a surprise.

So we agreed we'd meet at home in a few hours. I went downstairs and filled in the time puttering around until she returned. I heard the car pull into the driveway and began anticipating.

She'll come right down. I know it.

Well, she came in. But she went directly . . . upstairs. I heard her go. So I banged a hammer a couple of times just to make sure she would know where I was.

Now she'll come for sure.

I could see it. My wife would come down to the basement, fall into my arms, and tell me how good it was to have me home.

But she didn't.

Well, how do you like that? I decided not to budge. *After all, I had traveled all that distance, just to be with her and the kids. Wouldn't you think she would come down and tell me how good it was for me to be home?*

But she didn't.

I was really mad. Mind you, less than twenty-four hours earlier, I had been teaching people how to walk in the spirit of love . . . how to have patience, long-suffering.

Finally, I stomped upstairs. She was getting lunch ready and gave me only a cold shoulder.

If she doesn't want to talk to me, I'm certainly not going to talk to her. I was huffing and puffing inside.

We sat down to a miserable lunch. I glared at her. She glared at me. Finally, I got up from the table and went into the living room, feeling that certainly she would come in and sit down with me.

Know what she did?

She started up the sewing machine! And there I sat, a smoldering keg of temperamental dynamite, finally blurting:

"Will you shut off that sewing machine? I traveled clear across the country to come home and you don't pay attention to me!"

"What do you mean?" she snapped back.

"Well, I'm home, and you're sewing."

"Did you just get home?" She was blazing now. "Why didn't you come up to see me? You didn't have to stay in the basement!"

How about that? I was downstairs simmering. She was upstairs simmering. I was thinking that the least she could do was come down and see me. She was thinking:

If he can fly 2,000 miles to see me, then how come he can't walk up the stairs?

58

Can you believe it? Two grown-up people acting like that?

God's love was missing. Love does not act unbecoming, because it does not seek its own, and therefore is not easily provoked. We really flunked that test.

What do justified people do when they realize they are wrong? The Bible tells us:

> If we walk in the light as He Himself is in the light, we have fellowship with one another, and the blood of Jesus His Son cleanses us from all sin (1 John 1:7).

The foolishness of our behavior hit both of us like a light and we confessed our sins (unbecoming behavior, self-seeking, become provoked) to God and let Him bathe our hearts once again with His love. Our fellowship was restored.

The love of God turns you into a person who is watchful, careful, and sensitive to the people around you. Without it, you turn back to self-seeking.

Love does not act unbecoming, does not seek its own, is not easily provoked.

LOVE DOES NOT TAKE INTO ACCOUNT A WRONG SUFFERED . . . LOVE DOES NOT REJOICE IN UNRIGHTEOUSNESS . . .

There are some common "wrongs" that occur over and over. We are all familiar with the following:

* A husband doesn't allow enough time for his wife and friends
* A wife neglects her husband and family
* One partner is financially irresponsible
* Emotional or physical involvement with someone else
* Wife doesn't cook or keep house to suit her husband
* One partner indulges or pampers the children
* The offended partner retaliates

There is a "real wrong" involved — no doubt about it. The sad part is that the *innocent party* often ends up in the consulting room, angry, bitter, and resentful.

"Why not?" is the normal question fired at me.

There is a better way. Respond with God's love (patient, long-suffering, kind). You still have the problem, but you work on it without suffering. Remember that anger, resentment, and bitterness in the innocent party do not bother the one who is wrong.

Isn't it great to know that God's love is available to you when you need it the most — when you are wronged?

The other side of the coin would be to rejoice in unrighteousness. Perhaps your partner has lectured you on your unacceptable behavior and now is doing the same thing. You're glad.

Someone else's children are in trouble, and you're happy. You deliberately come home late and smugly enjoy it when your partner loses his or her temper.

The love of God in you doesn't stop because of a wrong suffered. Nor do you enjoy seeing someone else doing wrong or enjoy retaliating wrongly yourself.

Love does not take into account wrong suffered, does not rejoice in unrighteousness.

LOVE REJOICES WITH THE TRUTH

Every morning you wake up with some facts to face. These include memories of yesterday, the demands of today, and the unknowns of tomorrow. Let's look at some:

married or unmarried	pretty or not pretty
children or no children	educated or uneducated
alone or with someone	rich or poor
strong or weak	employed or unemployed
tall or short	treated well or mistreated
sick or well	

Before you get out of bed, you can let the love of God bathe your heart. Then you can rejoice in these truths (and others) — bear all things, believe all things, hope all things, endure all things — without taking into account wrongs suffered or contemplating unrighteous choices.

You can accept yourself — the positives and negatives.

Take Paul for instance. He would like to be 6' 4", weigh 240 pounds, and be a linebacker for a professional football team. Instead, every morning, when he plants his feet on the floor, he must face the fact he is 5' 5'' and weighs 138 pounds.

Floyd is a builder. He has several hundred thousand dollars worth of projects underway. The building trades are on strike, so he is unable to complete his projects. The interest on his loans for the projects are eating up his capital. Floyd faces the real possibility of bankruptcy.

Jean has three preschool children. Today, they all have colds.

Betty has a boy whom she loves dearly. He is nineteen and has left home. She doesn't know where he is or what he is doing.

John looks out the window, staring vacantly at nothing. He is strong and healthy. And unemployed. He would rather work than draw unemployment, but he has no choice.

Bob has just received divorce papers from his wife's lawyer. He realizes he asked for it by pouring his life into his work and his golf game, while ignoring his family. His drinking made his company undesirable when he did come home.

Everyone faces a set of daily truths. You have yours, and I mine. God's love helps us to accept unchangeable circumstances and helps us to enjoy working on them.

SPEAKING THE TRUTH

There is another kind of truth, involving the thoughts, opinions, and behavior of other people.

"I wouldn't dare give all my opinions or reveal all my thoughts," says one of my clients. "My partner would be upset, feel hurt, hold a grudge, or would never forgive me."

How true. Communication often is cut off when one partner does not "rejoice with the truth."

Susan and Eric illustrate this. Eric had to face the truth about Susan's housekeeping and her reactions to his opinions. Susan had to face Eric's opinions about her choices and his subsequent reactions. Neither Eric nor Susan rejoiced with the truth. Rather, the truth exposed deception, hatred, resentment, rebellion, self-centeredness, impatience.

Healthy marriages are built on the cornerstone of

rejoicing in the truth. You enjoy hearing what your partner is thinking. It gives you a realistic picture of your relationship. Love rejoices with the truth.

LOVE BEARS ALL THINGS

The word "bear" is used here as a covering (or roof) that keeps the rain out and the heat in. It contains and keeps things from spilling out.

As you face life's difficulties, God's love helps you contain heartaches, pains, bruises, suffering, and problems without spilling over on other people. This love enables you to wait for the family conference. You don't have to spill everything out right now — if you are really loving.

Alton's boss bawled him out unmercifully in front of his associates. Alton took it with a smile, but nursed a growing hatred toward his boss.

This hatred spilled over at home. He jumped on his wife as his boss had jumped on him. He took an occasional swat at his small child all out of proportion to the circumstances. With God's love, Alton's smile would have reflected a genuine kindly spirit, rather than hide his hatred. Then he could have enjoyed his family.

Let me share one of my favorite Bible passages with you. It has cured many aching marriages.

> But the wisdom from above is first pure, then peaceable, gentle, reasonable, full of mercy and good fruits, unwavering, without hypocrisy. And the seed whose fruit is righteousness is sown in peace by those who make peace (James 3:17,18).

We all have problems, but God's love makes either a gentleman or a lady out of us. You can bear your own burdens without spilling on others who are uninterested or can't help. Free from envy and strife, you can think straight. For consultation, you turn to a lawyer, a physician, a counselor, or a friend. Now, tackling problems can be a pleasure and joy.

LOVE BELIEVES ALL THINGS

With this attitude, you accept the best in people as long as possible.

Bill and Karen married a few days after they graduated from high school. His job as a supermarket stock boy didn't pay much, but they loved each other.

"That's what counts," they agreed.

They were soon deep in debt. Then, the other shoe fell. Bill was fired for loafing.

The next ten years were a succession of rough experiences. Bill enrolled in college, and Karen went to work. Halfway through the semester, he quit. He lost a succession of jobs: truckdriver, tool shop worker, vacuum cleaner salesman, and insurance salesman.

Two children were born. As soon as possible, in both cases, Karen was back at work. Bill, however, loafed around the house, causing their families and friends to write him off.

Karen had days when she was ready to leave, but she found Jesus and His love. She wavered at times but always repented and asked God to restore her belief in her husband and renew her patience. Meanwhile she encouraged, urged, and pressured Bill.

Finally, Bill was working as a fry cook, night shift. That's about all you can expect of him, everyone thought. Things were different this time. Like a butterfly, Bill emerged from his cocoon.

In quick succession, he was on days . . . then in charge of the kitchen . . . then in charge of training cooks for this restaurant chain . . . then in charge of food management for the chain . . . then owning his own restaurant. Today, Bill is a respected, prosperous businessman.

It was a long, long road for Karen. But God's love had sustained her. Love believes all things — even for ten years.

"You can't trust anyone," Jerome growled at me, basing his judgment on two traumatic incidents. Several years ago his wife ran off with one of his friends. A dozen years ago, another "friend" skipped town and left him to pay off a note Jerome had co-signed.

When I told him that with God's love he could again believe in people, Jerome exploded with rage and stomped out of the consulting room to nurse his grudges. Of course, he was seriously wronged, but his rage didn't bother the people who wronged him. They didn't even know where he was. He was the architect of his own suffering.

To be sure, there are untrustworthy people. After you've done everything possible to establish a person's integrity and they still mislead, God's love will sustain your faith in other people.

Love believes all things.

LOVE HOPES ALL THINGS

Harold risked all he had in a business venture. It was going beautifully until the economy dipped. Instead of having rosy prospects, Harold was deeply in debt and without an income.

He had two options. He could turn on himself, bemoan his situation, and berate himself. This he did for a while.

No one cares about me, especially God. And . . . that's what I get for believing in free enterprise.

Or Harold could scurry back to God and let Him renew his spirit. This he did next. What a change in his thoughts!

I may be bankrupt, and that's bad. But I'm not sick, and that's good. I am bankrupt and unemployed. That's double bad. Regardless, I still have a family, and that's good. I have an education and some ability. That's double good.

With his hope in God renewed, Harold tackled his problems. Nothing changed with the snap of two fingers. Creditors hounded him unmercifully. Two years later, he was back on the track. Now, he has a good job and is slowly repaying his creditors. Sustained by hope in God, he's experienced something that ruined other men.

There was no easy way out. But no matter what people said, or what he heard, Harold's hope spurred him on. He almost crossed himself off. But, God's love . . .

Love hopes all things.

LOVE ENDURES ALL THINGS

It was Jesus who said:

These things I have spoken to you, that in Me you may have peace. In the world you have tribulation, but take courage; I have overcome the world (John 16:33).

We cringe in the face of financial crises, sickness, mistreatments, misunderstandings, rejection, and persecution. Our inner response is the problem. Self-seeking and the deeds of the flesh cause suffering.

However, the person who looks forward to each day with a zest for living understands that life involves facing one problem after another. Part of the fun of living is to look forward to the next problem and the challenge of working it out with the love of God in your heart.

Love endures all things.

LOVE NEVER FAILS

What kind of love never fails? It is God's love. Let's review what that love is:

patient	does not rejoice in
kind	unrighteousness
not jealous	rejoices in truth
not arrogant	bears all things
does not seek its own	believes all things
is not provoked	hopes all things
does not take into	endures all things
account wrongs suffered	never fails

PROMISES THAT MISS THE MARK

During courtship, all couples reassure each other: *Love will carry us through. Let's get married.* Yet as I have pressed troubled couples to define love, they usually answer:

"A tender feeling; a thrilling response to hugs and kisses; sexual relations; tender words and promises; making an effort to please each other."

Alas, we soon discover that disagreements intensify self-seeking and deeds of the flesh as never before. They cool the thrill and ecstasy of physical contact, lead to harsh words, ill will, and open conflict.

Wait a minute!

My experience in the consulting room has taught me that the principles of chapter 4 and so far in chapter 5 throw up a red flag in people's minds. So let's raise the question I hear over and over:

"Do you mean that without God's help, marriage won't work? I know many couples who are getting along just fine who have *no* interest in God."

Let me ask you: how many people know what goes on between you and your partner? Many couples end up in my consulting room who appear to their friends to be doing just fine.

Rather than looking around at what you can observe in other couples, let me urge you to be guided by what you know about your own marriage.

You have sincerely tried to stir up tender feelings and an atmosphere of good will. But you missed it.

WHEN YOU NEED LOVE THE MOST!

God's love can bind you together. Review that list of elements. Memorize it. It will restore the thrill of hugging and kissing, the warmth of friendship.

When do you need the love of God the most? Usually, when you don't want it — *during* the problem, *while* the discussion is going on, *when* you are being ignored, *if* the decision goes against you.

Remember Ken and Nancy? She had been unmarried for so many years she was looking forward to the "freedom and fellowship" of marriage. Unlimited sexual satisfaction. Continuous fellowship.

Just think! I'll never be alone again. It will be perfect.

Yet, when Nancy got to Florida, she was so unhappy she took the next flight home. Nancy needed God's love when Ken ignored her. He wouldn't have ignored her if that love had filled him.

Eric needed it when Susan failed to see the cobwebs for seven days. Susan needed it when Eric came up with his unexpected and unwelcome ideas.

Like many couples, one of their first reactions was to change their partner or get out of their partner's presence. Just get away from the whole mess. It was all a mistake.

Right?

Wrong!

Couples in trouble need the love of God. They still face the same problems, but God helps them respond differently. The love of God eliminates the friction, allowing them to resolve their differences.

Your negative response results from the absence of God's love, not from the presence or choices of your partner.

> May the Lord cause you to increase and abound in love for one another, and for all men, just as we also do for you (1 Thess. 3:12).

A NEW OPTION

What do you do when you're not drawing upon the love of God? You admit your mistake, then recall God's promise in Romans 5:5:

> The love of God has been poured out within our hearts through the Holy Spirit who was given to us.

Then you ask Him to restore that missing element of God's love. You let God give you His love when you need it. The choice is yours.

Try it.

Let God bathe your heart with His kind of love (recheck the list). Then you'll get on with making your marriage better.

6 / The Hottest Question Facing Marriage Partners — Leadership

6 / The Hottest Question Facing Marriage Partners — Leadership

IT'S A TOUCHY QUESTION

Probably the touchiest, most controversial question of all in marriage is our next subject: leadership.

To put it simply: who is the boss?

Why do two married people who have the love of God in their hearts need a leader? Because when a decision must be made, however small, and when opinions differ, *there is no other way to settle it.*

A leader is necessary whenever two or more people must cooperate. Take tennis for example.

A GAME OF SINGLES . . . ?

In singles, you have your own side of the court all to yourself. You do anything you please within the rules, without consulting or considering anyone else. You can charge the net, play back, to the right, or left. You do your own thing. The idea is to outplay, outsmart, outmaneuver each other. You win or lose.

And, it's fun to compete.

. . . OR DOUBLES?

Suppose you and your best friend team up to play doubles. When you hop over the net, it's the same court, same equipment, same players.

But a different game. Now you cooperate instead

of compete. You're teammates instead of opponents and you can only partially do your own thing. You would collide if you both went after the ball. If you were both in the same place, your opponents would place the ball out of your reach.

In order to play smoothly together, you choose a captain. Together you work out a strategy: who plays right, who plays left. Most of these decisions are obvious. You combine your skills. If there is a question, the captain calls the shots. It's fun to cooperate.

Without cooperation and a leader, you can't successfully play doubles. *One of the doubles partners must have the last word when opinions differ.*

Courtship is like playing singles. You are good friends. You discuss, even debate, many subjects — money, cars, politics, goals, values, neatness, dress, religion, just about anything. You especially enjoy it when you end up on opposite sides of a subject without disturbing each other's good will.

Both freely express opinions. *You don't have to reach an agreement.*

"BEFORE MARRIAGE . . . WE COULD DISCUSS ANYTHING!"

Then you get married. The same subjects come up for discussion: money, cars, goals, values, neatness, dress, religion. But now it's different. I've heard many couples say:

"We could discuss anything before we were married. Now we quarrel half the time."

Exactly.

Before you were married, all you had to do was discuss. Now you must decide. Before, you could end the discussion and go your own way — just like playing your half of the court in singles.

When you marry, you not only discuss questions or issues, you must come to agreements and cooperate. You can only partially do your own thing.

IN TENNIS — THE RULES ARE SET

It is at the point of decision-making — when opinions differ and cannot be resolved — that one of you must have the last word. Purpose? To settle the issue.

Opinions differ. This was true of Eric and Susan, Henry and Eva, Ken and Nancy. It happens to people with the loftiest of motives, in and out of marriage.

If you play doubles in tennis, it's fun if decisions are agreeable and can be made quickly and easily. This can be done if you have some guidelines and a captain.

In tennis, the guidelines are the tennis court and the rules. *These already exist and cannot be changed.* You determine how you cooperate on the court and within the rules.

You need a captain to call the shots when there is a question. *Choosing the captain is up to the two of you.* If you can't work out a choice, you won't enjoy playing doubles.

IN MARRIAGE — THE RULES ARE CREATED

Launching a marriage differs from launching a tennis doubles team. And you come into marriage from two different backgrounds. The husband's family had a different set of rules than his wife's.

Now the two of you must do something you've probably never done before: create your own boundaries, rules, and leadership style. You probably don't have any previous experience to prepare you for this. You may have no idea how to set up boundaries and rules, much less live by them.

You probably thought two married people in love automatically got along.

Sharon and John thought they could talk things over and come to agreeable solutions. Although complete opposites, they were enjoying being in love.

John was consistently punctual. When he said eight o'clock, he meant eight-zero-zero. Sharon was always late. So John sat there and fumed disgustedly.

Then . . . the grand entrance.

Down the steps came Sharon. All loveliness. Her figure, beautiful eyes, sparkling smile . . . all something to behold.

She bounded across the room, her inviting arms outstretched. Suddenly, John forgot his griping.

His whole body experienced a pleasant sensation as she touched his hand. Then Sharon would cuddle up to John, and all he could see ahead of him was a wonderful evening — with a delightful girl.

Occasionally, while they were sitting alone talking, he asked her:

"Honey, are you going to be late like this after we're married?" Sharon would cuddle up to John, look up at him seductively, and say:

"Would it really matter to you if I were late after we got married? Wouldn't you love me anyway?"

"Honey," he would say in a burst of daring confidence, "I'd love you no matter what you did!"

So the punctual young man married the wistful maiden of his dreams, promising to love her no matter what!

When John woke up the first morning after the honeymoon, he bounded out of bed at the first ring of the alarm and, minutes later, emerged from the bathroom washed, shaved, dressed, and ready for breakfast.

But where was his wife?

He did a double take. *She was still in bed!*

"C'mon! C'mon!" he called to his sweetheart. "Aren't you going to make my breakfast?" From beneath the covers came a sleepy sigh:

"You can get something at the donut shop, can't you?"

She had her own schedule and wasn't in that much of a hurry. But he pressured her more every day. When they were getting ready to go anywhere he pushed her and offered time checks until her nerves nearly snapped. This same couple had said only a few months earlier:

"We're the perfect couple. One's punctual, the other's late. We'll balance each other. We'll even improve each other."

It sounded reasonable. But now John had interpreted her pokiness as a subtle feminine whack at his masculine authority. She saw his pushiness as unnecessary nagging.

There were other disagreements — and all followed a pattern. John would fume a few days, then bring up

74

the subject. Sharon would cuddle up to him, ask him to declare his love for her, then keep on doing her own thing. John would contain himself a few days, then force another discussion and angrily spill out his opinion.

Sharon would counter. After a few exchanges, the conversation would grind to a disgusted silence with no solution.

Every attempt ended in a hopeless deadlock, and Sharon and John made the same mistake thousands of other married couples have. *They arrived at the tragic conclusion they were mismatched.*

"He doesn't understand me," Sharon sobbed.

"She doesn't care about me," came John's snarling reply.

Only a few months earlier, he had tingled all over just thinking about Sharon. And she had happily melted into those big, strong arms and stood on tiptoe to kiss him lingeringly. Now, they couldn't stand to touch each other.

Declaring their love and wanting to get along hadn't created harmonious relations. Nor had the ecstasy of sexual relations. Instead, self-seeking and the deeds of the flesh (resentment and anger) had cooled the thrill of physical contact and thrown up a wall between them.

THERE IS A WAY OUT

Sharon and John turned with me to the Bible for guidance. We studied the same material you did in chapters 4 and 5 of this book. They agreed they needed the love of God (patience, kindness, does not seek its own, is not provoked) to create a climate for dealing with their deadlocks. The result? They again enjoyed the thrill of physical contact and the warmth of friendship.

They still face the same problems, with or without the love of God. But the friction is eliminated with the love of God that allows them to find a way out of their differences. The process means years of sacrifice and hard work for both of them.

THE BIG THREE

We leave Sharon and John, and turn to the Bible

for guidance in making a marriage better. We will coin a term: *three keys to harmonious marriage.*

These keys are some of the most hotly debated principles in the Bible. If followed, however, they provide the basis for defining the guidelines and rules to help make your marriage better. We assume you are a child of God with the love of God in your heart. Without this as a starting point, we give you no hope.

COOPERATION — THE FIRST KEY

> Be subject to one another in the fear of Christ (Eph. 5:21).

In other words, you intend to cooperate. You will work together to discover areas of agreement and disagreement. You are committed to seriously consider your partner's interests as you seek a meeting of minds.

SUBMISSION — THE SECOND KEY

> Wives, be subject to your own husbands, as to the Lord (Eph. 5:22).

We've repeated that any two or more people who must cooperate, no matter how friendly or dedicated, will sooner or later encounter differences of opinion that lead finally to a deadlock. Someone *must* settle these. In marriage, it's the husband. Submission is the most hotly debated issue in marriage.

COMMITMENT — THE THIRD KEY

> For the husband is the head of the wife, as Christ also is the head of the church, He Himself being the Savior of the body (Eph. 5:23).

These are heavy words. If the husband is to conduct himself toward his wife as Christ did toward the church, we had better take a good look at what Christ did for the church. We know that Jesus served the church and even died for it.

NO OTHER WAY

These three keys will enable your marriage to endure. There is no other way. We will examine them more closely in the next three chapters.

7 / Cooperation: The First Key (Partners . . . Not Opponents)

7 / Cooperation: The First Key (Partners . . . Not Opponents)

COOPERATION: THE FIRST KEY

> Be subject to one another in the fear of Christ (Eph. 5:21).
>
> Do not merely look out for your own personal interests, but also for the interests of others (Phil. 2:4).

One of the joys of my life is helping couples turn the word "submission" from a rather disturbing word into a warm, friendly, satisfying word.

It is the will to cooperate . . . loyalty . . . good-natured tolerance.

It's pleasant to listen to a couple describe their marriage when cooperation, like-mindedness, and agreement exist. Their eyes shine, their voices ring with satisfaction, even their skin glows.

On the other hand, when couples describe disagreement, discord, or conflict, I watch faces turn white, red, blue, purple. I listen to angry, vicious verbal tirades or observe hostile silence.

Their backs stiffen, jaws become set, and eyes become slits.

COOPERATION IS PLEASANT

Once more, let's compare a marriage partnership with playing doubles in tennis.

Part of the fun of doubles is good will and friendship, a willingness to play according to the rules, and the will to develop teamwork.

In doubles, you blend your skill. One partner may have a good forehand, the other a good backhand. This determines your playing position on the court, but then it takes weeks and months of practice to develop a cooperative style.

You work independently as well as cooperatively. When the ball is in your area you are on your own. You make good and poor shots, causing your partner to admire — or tolerate — your efforts. You make quick decisions, according to your agreed-upon plan. At times it may be necessary to alter your plan.

It is pleasant to look forward to a tennis match that may be days away. The actual match may last only an hour, but the rewards of playing together are worth all the effort.

It is no fun if one partner doesn't try, or if you fight over how to cooperate, or over who is the captain.

SUBMISSION — A PLEASANT WORD

Submission means pleasure if you meet the conditions:
* Good will and friendship
* Pleasant anticipation
* The will to play by the rules
* The will to choose a captain
* The will to develop teamwork between you
To put it in a Bible verse:

Be subject to one another in the fear of Christ (Eph. 5:21).

Now, let's switch from cooperation in tennis to cooperation in marriage.

A FIRM FOUNDATION

What do you have to start with? Consider this list:
1. You are a child of God
2. You have the love of God in your heart
3. You have made a commitment to each other
4. You mean to cooperate

COOPERATION: THE FIRST KEY

REMEMBER THOSE VOWS?

Remember your wedding ceremony? The vows went something like this:

> Dearly beloved, we are gathered together in the sight of God . . .

Marriage is *God's* idea. Remember His words?

> The LORD God said: "It is not good for the man to be alone; I will make him a helper suitable for him" (Gen. 2:18).

Then you declared your intentions toward each other even further:

> Will you love her, comfort her, honor and keep her . . . in sickness and in health; and forsaking all others, keep thee only unto her so long as you both shall live . . . ?

> I . . . take you . . . to have and to hold, from this day forward, for better, for worse, for richer, for poorer, in sickness and in health, to love and to cherish, till death us do part . . . .

That ceremony suggests that:

1. You are ready to start with each other as you are, not pending reform.

2. You will love and respect each other in spite of your shortcomings.

3. You will continue to work for the success of the marriage.

4. Disagreements are normal and expected but shouldn't be allowed to ruin the marriage.

5. This is an exclusive relationship. "Forsaking all others," the marriage comes first.

> For this cause [she is suitable for him] a man shall leave his father and his mother, and shall cleave to his wife; and they shall become one flesh (Gen. 2:24).

6. You permanently commit yourselves to this marriage.

THE STARTING POINT

Perhaps you haven't yet made such vows — or if you have you haven't taken them seriously. Either way, if you expect to make your marriage better, such a commitment is needed now as a starting point.

In chapter 4 of this book, we discussed the basis for

good human relations. It's similar to your marriage vows:

> Make my joy complete by being of the same mind, maintaining the same love, united in spirit, intent on one purpose. Do nothing from selfishness or empty conceit, but with humility of mind let each of you regard one another as more important than himself; do not merely look out for your own personal interests, but also for the interests of others (Phil. 2:2-4).

Here's what these verses say:

1. You intend to come to a meeting of minds.
2. You consider your partner as important as yourself.
3. You intend to look out for your partner's interests as well as your own.

Doesn't this sound great? Such a foundation must exist to succeed. There is more:

> Have this attitude in yourselves which was also in Christ Jesus, who, although He existed in the form of God, did not regard equality with God a thing to be grasped, but emptied Himself, taking the form of a bond-servant, and being made in the likeness of men. And being found in appearance as a man, He humbled Himself by becoming obedient to the point of death, even death on a cross (Phil. 2:5-8).

What do these verses say?

1. You intend to serve one another.
2. Both partners will comply with decisions made by the partnership (obedience).

That is being subject to each other in the fear of Christ. That is cooperation.

BUILDING ON YOUR COMMITMENT — DECIDING ON THE GUIDELINES

In marriage, like playing doubles in tennis, each partner must make many independent decisions. So, the first and most difficult decisions facing a newly married couple involve dividing up responsibilities and setting up guidelines and rules that will help you make mutually agreeable decisions as you act independently.

The need for new guidelines, or revising the ones you have set up, will gradually unfold as weeks and months go by. This means many little meetings together, called by either one of you, as the need arises.

COOPERATION: THE FIRST KEY

CAUTION!

    1. Decision-making is the name of the game.

    2. There will be intelligent decisions and dumb ones.

    3. To make the best possible decisions, both partners must lay their likes, dislikes, ambitions, goals, interests, abilities, and thoughts on the table.

    4. The meetings must be regular, whether formal or informal.

    5. Generalizations or statistics about what "men" are like or what "women" are like will not serve you here.

    6. What is important is for you to know what *your* partner is like.

WARNING!

    Some people are reluctant to disrobe and reveal their bodies in front of their partners. It is even more difficult to disrobe mentally and emotionally, so to speak, before your partner. You don't want to offend or reveal ideas and thoughts that might be held against you. Also, you might not be able to handle what your partner reveals.

    I am not suggesting that this process will be easy or completed in an evening. There will be surprises — and delays — in deciding.

    Read the list again: likes, dislikes, ambitions, goals, interests, abilities, thoughts. These gradually unfold over months, even years. And they will change.

    Promises, commitments, agreements made today may not make sense at all next year. Decision-making is a process that goes on and on as long as we live.

    For example, after making a *sincere* effort to please your partner, you announce that you don't really like what you are doing.

    "Yeah, I went with you to a few concerts when we were dating, but I don't really like concerts."

    "You don't like concerts?"

    Or . . . "Well, I went with you to those basketball games when we were dating, but I really don't get excited about sports."

"What? Run that by me again."

Your partner might suddenly announce he or she doesn't enjoy going to church, wants to change jobs, would like to move from the area. Anything might come up.

Take the warning. This process of decision-making can be risky and explosive. From what's on the table — the information about yourselves and the decisions to be made — you forge mutually agreed-upon choices.

What could be more fun than two people, who care about each other and want to please each other, planning for the future?

And remember . . . all in the presence of God.

Without God's love and a sincere desire to consider the interests of your partner, decision-making becomes intolerable. With God's love you can build on a foundation of commitment and develop the best plan possible for this most important partnership.

THE AGENDA

You can't cover everything in one evening. Some decisions involve more discussion than you thought they needed. Others might have to wait for another day. Few decisions *must* be made today.

Love is patient.

You divide responsibilities according to ability, interests, likes, and dislikes. Who will handle the fund raising? The purchasing? The accounting? The cooking? Who will make decisions in case of a deadlock?

You may have taken a responsibility your partner could have done better or easier. So, you negotiate a swap. Each partner must handle some responsibilities that can't be exchanged, whether you like them or not. Then, there are decisions about church, social life, in-laws.

We're talking about continuous, ongoing meetings, necessary because of constant changes. For instance . . .

. . . he had accepted the bookkeeping job, but she can do it more accurately and faster, so she took over that one.

. . . he originally agreed to go shopping with his wife. After a while they scrapped that idea, for she didn't really need his company while shopping.

Agreements and assigned responsibilities are not cast in concrete. They can be changed. It is not:

"Look, let's get this organized so we don't have to have any more meetings." The meetings will continue throughout your marriage. It is not:

"You promised me two years ago, and I'm holding you to it for life."

In a business partners develop policies, procedures, and rules. They make changes necessary to accomplish the objectives of the business. They observe how responsibility and authority are handled, and if everyone is well placed. They even note who can take on more responsibility.

Marriage involves the same process. And you *both* must be actively involved. Discussions may take place.

While driving in the car, sitting at the kitchen table, in the living room or bedroom, on the patio — anywhere.

In a nutshell, both husband and wife should be expected to participate vigorously and forthrightly in the search for mutually agreeable decisions.

That's submission.

CAUSE FOR DISORDER

Remember, the discussion goes on in the atmosphere of the love of God (it would be a good idea to review chapters 4 and 5). If this spirit is missing in either partner, then table the issue. Get your hearts straightened out. Your attitude is a personal matter between you and God. You can come back to the issue another day. A key Bible verse is important here:

> For where jealousy and selfish ambition exist, there is disorder and every evil thing (James 3:16).

COME BACK TO THE ISSUE . . .

You need to come back to the issue when you have tabled a decision. Don't let it fester too long. Once you are filled with the love of God, you can review the facts of the tabled item and settle it. Your marriage is too important to be making decisions without the love of God in your heart.

Love bears and endures all things. An unresolved issue or a decision different from yours does not separate you from the love of God.

As often as not, the husband is the one who is determined to make an unreasonable, foolish, or selfish decision.

After all, a woman shouldn't be expected to pretend agreement if her judgment differs from her husband's. He should have the benefit of her opinion and she needs his.

Generally, differences between couples don't center on issues where a decision is clearly wrong. Rather, the issue is a matter of opinion, and the decision could go either way.

The question is: *Whose way?*

THE WIFE SHOULD EXPRESS HER JUDGMENT . . .

In marriage, the wife has a half interest in the partnership. Her stake is *equal* to her husband's. Her judgment and experience is needed to make many of the decisions. She should be expected to do all she can to influence the direction of the partnership — to participate vigorously in the decision-making.

If she disagrees with her husband's views, she should say so. He should know whether or not she has changed her mind. And she needs to know what is on her husband's mind.

Together, a couple works at finding a mutually agreeable decision.

Agreement on a *family plan* (not "Joe's plan" . . . or "Mary's plan") is where cooperation begins. Then it takes daily effort, constant examination, and frequent changes to keep it going.

THOSE TWO-TONED SHOES

Without guidelines and the love of God in your hearts, you become candidates for the consulting room.

That's where I met Lars and Carol. Lars was an impressive man. And did he ever have a beautiful wife!

She was gorgeous. You looked at her and said: "Wow!"

And that's what I was thinking to myself when I suddenly did a double take. Could this really be true? Sure enough, this lovely lass had a black eye.

Lars had done it.

It had all started one Thursday. Lars woke up in an ugly mood. Mind you, this man was a college graduate and had a good job. The family lived in a fine house and went to church every week. Yet, that Thursday, Lars woke up in an ugly mood. How come? His explanation:

"I'm like that."

He assumed that if you are like that, there was nothing you could do about it — certainly not change.

Lars and Carol had been married long enough to have four children. Lars knew Carol was going downtown that day to buy shoes, so he made a little speech at breakfast:

"Now, listen here," he said, glaring at his wife. "I want you to get something straight! I know you are going downtown today to buy shoes.

"I don't mind you buying black shoes, brown shoes, even white shoes, but I don't want you coming home with any two-toned shoes, do you understand?"

Carol had made up her mind what she would do before he got halfway through that speech. She was already thinking . . .

So help me, I'm going downtown and coming home with four pairs of two-toned shoes.

She hadn't intended to do that, but his speech made her angry and rebellious.

Her logic was that any woman who got talked to like Lars had talked to her was not responsible for her decisions.

Would you buy that idea?

By now, I suppose most of our readers have taken sides.

Well, she bought the shoes, came home, caught the kids, and put the shoes on them. By the time Lars came home that evening, those shoes had three hours of wear. They were used shoes.

She won round two.

Round three was coming — three days later. And, believe it or not, Lars (remember . . . a college graduate, nice big house, good job and all) again woke up in an ugly mood.

On a Sunday morning!

Could you believe it?

That was bad enough, but another drama was about to unfold. His gorgeous wife had pulled four pairs of two-toned shoes out of their respective closets and put them in the basement, where every Sunday morning it was dad's responsibility to shine them.

So Lars went down to the basement — in an ugly mood.

And things got uglier.

Imagine the scene. An angry father was facing four scuffed-up pairs of two-toned shoes.

Glaring at them.

Then he started polishing them. Can you predict what kind of a job he's going to do?

Sure enough, he got some black on the white of the first shoe. When he was finished with the first pair of shoes, he gave them to the rightful owner. The child ran up the stairs, and Carol's reaction to Lars' efforts echoed down the stairs.

"Is that the best your father can do?"

Wow!

Try to picture him now. He grits his teeth and finishes the second and third pairs. Now, three children have shoes polished. But Carol notices one shoeless child.

Downstairs, a very angry dad is working on the fourth pair of shoes, when his wife's voice comes downstairs again.

"Isn't your father finished yet?"

Bingo! He starts polishing with a vengeance. He finishes the fourth pair and stomps up the stairs. At the head of the stairs stands his wife, looking down her nose at him.

Can you see her? Defiant. Resolute. Every inch of her body taking him on. She fires out at him:

"About time!" A nasty glint in her eye.

And that's when he let her have it. Right in the eye. Have you ever done that?

Let me ask you men another question. Have you ever considered doing it? Some of you ladies may not know how close you've come to that black eye.

Well, Lars hadn't done this before either. There is always a first time for everything, and what Lars did was *to send his wife sprawling on the kitchen floor.*

At least he helped her up. And they finally agreed on something . . . that she had a bad eye.

They were two shocked people as they told me their story. What was wrong?

PLAYING SINGLES

1. The love of God was missing.
2. They had no guidelines.
3. They were not committed to cooperation.

Lars was a hostile, self-seeking man. When he lashed out angrily at Carol he got her fighting mad and rebellious. They were opponents, not teammates. All these years, decision-making was a contest. When he won, she lost. If she won, he lost.

When I pointed this out to them, they agreed on something else: they were both angry at me.

In chapter 4, we noted that marriage magnifies, rather than eliminates, your sins. What were Lars' and Carol's sins? Hostility, self-seeking, rebellion.

But people cool off. So did Lars and Carol. Later, they recalled my little speech and admitted it was true.

They did repent, became children of God, and let Him bathe their hearts with His love.

CHANGE TO PLAYING DOUBLES

Two people as intelligent as Lars and Carol could carry on from there without my help. They were quite capable of working out their own objectives, policies, procedures, and rules.

SIX REASONS . . .

Across the years, there will be many conferences.

Either partner can call the meeting for any of these reasons:

1. To set a policy or a rule
2. To make some changes
3. To report a problem
4. To report on progress
5. Because one isn't carrying out his or her responsibility
6. To express praise and admiration for a partner's performance

Actually, most decisions will be obvious. There will also be tough questions with no easy answers. The result? Unresolved deadlocks.

There is a way to handle them, too.

8 / Submission: The Second Key (The Tie-Breaker)

8 / Submission: The Second Key (The Tie-Breaker)

SUBMISSION: THE SECOND KEY

> Wives, be subject to your own husbands, as to the Lord (Eph. 5:22).

Ouch. There it is. The most hotly debated Bible verse concerning marriage.

"Why should the wife do all the submitting?" That's the hot question.

She doesn't have to.

This verse doesn't stand alone. Remember the one before it?

> Be subject to one another in the fear of Christ (Eph. 5:21).

And another:

> Do not merely look out for your own personal interests, but also for the interests of others (Phil. 2:4).

IT HAPPENS BETWEEN FRIENDS

When does this hot issue surface? The matter of submission arises when opinions differ over a decision even with all facts on the table. Still neither you nor your partner gives in. Both get nasty. Good will and cooperation go out the window.

IT HAPPENS IN BUSINESS

Ned and Lorne had been friends for years. Both

were skilled toolmakers and had held executive positions. Across the years, they talked often about their work and developed respect and admiration for each other.

Both had saved large sums from their huge salaries. They pooled their savings and purchased a fine tool company.

A dream come true.

Now these fine, experienced, Christian gentlemen could pool their knowledge. It would be great fun to work as equal partners.

They had a nice, new building with an expensive conference room. Here they came for their idea sessions.

Soon, they realized they had some acute problems. They differed about handling employees. They were having trouble dividing up the responsibilities, and neither knew enough about accounting.

Their fancy conference room couldn't solve their problems. Even friendship, knowledge, experience, and dedication weren't enough to settle the differences.

Most of their problems resulted from having done things differently — and successfully — for years. Ned was used to giving instructions and expecting them to be carried out. He had been the boss. So had Lorne.

Now they were partners — with brilliant, but differing ideas. It wasn't a matter of right or wrong.

They were able to discuss their differences. They clearly defined and understood each other's viewpoints. But they deadlocked when it came to making decisions.

Honesty, understanding, respect, knowledge, and experience didn't settle the deadlocks. The theory that two friendly partners can each do their own thing wasn't working.

They were frustrated and disgusted. They had even had a few shouting matches, with both of them storming angrily out of their beautiful conference room — and ultimately into a consulting room.

THE BASIC PROBLEM

We agreed there were two basic problems: (1)

each turned to his own way (self-seeking) and (2) both needed God's love.

Sound familiar? So what should they do? Repent, ask God to forgive and bathe their hearts with His love. They needed a love that . . . is patient . . . does not seek its own . . . is not provoked . . . rejoices in the truth.

THE SPECIFIC PROBLEM

Ned and Lorne did this, but they still needed to resolve their differences. They went to an outside consultant who really dropped a bombshell: *they must choose a president who will then settle the disagreements.*

"But . . . but . . . we're equal partners."

"True. There's just no other way, however, to solve your disagreements. You also need outside help with your accounting."

A bitter pill to swallow, but it was either follow the advice or lose the business.

After weeks of agonizing, they chose Lorne president. They spent the next months dividing up responsibilities, developing policies and procedures both of them could live with.

Let's take a brief look at some of those conference room discussions. Both men preferred managing the shop over sales, advertising, purchasing, or supervising the office staff. But *all* the work had to be done. Without going into great detail, here is how they distributed the duties:

1. Ned managed the shop, personnel relations, and maintenance.

2. Lorne got sales, advertising, the office and engineering.

3. They divided purchasing. Ned made the purchases for the shop, Lorne everything else.

A POINT TO REMEMBER

As president, Lorne didn't make all the decisions. Ned capably managed his own area within the guidelines. Lorne capably handled his area.

They were still equal partners, both vitally interested in all areas of the business. They consulted each

other, reviewed any decisions they wished to, and participated equally in making them.

As a rule, Ned had the last word in the shop, with
Lorne contributing his knowledge. In his area, Lorne made
the decisions, with Ned as the resource person.

However, Lorne had the last word in any decision.
Rarely did he overrule Ned, but it did happen occasionally.
They once were deadlocked over whether to buy a new or
used machine. It almost killed Lorne to overrule his knowl-
edgeable friend, but there was no other way. They couldn't
argue endlessly over a machine.

The business grew and prospered. Ned and Lorne
enjoyed working together. They learned to know each other
better and developed confidence in each other's decision-
making ability — a process that took many months.

As Ned and Lorne reviewed their rocky beginning,
both admitted they were vaguely aware the question of the
last word would have to be settled. They had pushed the
question out of their thinking, hoping it would go away.
They both wanted to be president, but their pride made it
impossible for them to make the selection.

MANAGING YOUR MARRIAGE

Let's switch from Ned and Lorne to your marriage.

In chapter 7 we wrote at length about the
decision-making process in marriage. You are *equal*
partners. Responsibilities must be divided up. You need
policies, procedures, and rules in order to work cooperatively as well as independently.

Let's not soft-pedal the basic, hottest issue in marriage. *Deadlocks will happen.* All the facts can be on the
table and opinions still differ. Someone must have the last
word in order to settle a deadlock. According to the Bible, in
marriage *that someone is the husband.*

> Wives, be subject to your own husbands, as to the Lord (Eph.
> 5:22).

The husband doesn't make all the decisions. Remember, you are *equal* partners. You are both vitally interested in all areas of the marriage. As in a business, both

consult with each other, participate in making decisions and reviewing them.

The wife usually has the last word in her areas of responsibility. She is the decision-maker, her husband the resource person. In his area, the husband makes the decisions and his wife contributes her knowledge. Mostly, they work independently in their areas within mutually agreed-upon guidelines.

As the head, however, the husband has the last word in any decisions. Rarely does he overrule his wife, if both meet the conditions for cooperation. Do you remember them?

1. Good will and friendship
2. Pleasant anticipation
3. The will to live by the rules
4. The will to choose a leader
5. The will to develop teamwork

You'll enjoy working together as you know each other better and gain confidence in each other's decision-making ability. Developing faith and trust takes many months. Forging a new way of life from your different backgrounds takes time and patience.

To illustrate how a husband and wife practice submission to one another and to the head, here are three decisions made at our house.

WHAT WOULD YOU PAY FOR A STEREO?

Once my wife and I decided to buy a stereo. It would be a pleasant feature in our home. So we went shopping together, happily expecting to make an easy choice.

We looked at one for $70 and another for $700. One of us preferred the cheaper model, the other the expensive one.

We got so hung up on the decision, we tabled it until the next evening. It would be simple. The best viewpoint would win.

So we did just that.

Ladies before gentlemen, so she went first. I could hardly believe her presentation. Jumbled. No logic. No substance. How could she present such a feeble point of view? When my turn came, I was confident.

She'll be impressed with my presentation.

So I gave it. It was systematic. Considered all aspects. Boy, was it logical.

Funny thing, though.

She didn't think so. My presentation didn't convince her to change her point of view. We were deadlocked!

We were facing one of those situations in marriage where everything had been said that could be said. All the facts were in. Still, Eva and I were on opposite sides.

And it will happen to you. Regardless of how dedicated or friendly you are, there will be deadlocks like this in your marriage. It is a controversial issue, but must be settled.

THE LAST WORD . . .

Here comes the answer to how you settle a deadlock in a marriage. There is only one way. *The husband has the last word.* He has two options:

1. Make the decision himself.
2. Ask his wife to make it.

I settled the stereo deadlock by making the decision on which model we bought.

It is a grave, serious moment when Eva and I are deadlocked. She is as committed to this marriage as I am. She and I both want the best for the marriage. This is no time to be selfish or ignore her judgment.

It took a few days to ponder the issues, but the responsibility for making the decision was mine. Soon, we were past that decision and have enjoyed years of pleasant listening since.

THE KITCHEN EXPERT

Before we get too excited about the question of who has the last word, let's look at another decision.

We were moving into a new home and had to decide the layout and decor of the kitchen. We both agreed that I knew nothing about kitchens. Eva had been around them at least thirty-five years, and besides, she was the one who would use it.

Who do you think should have carried the ball on kitchen decisions? The answer was obvious — Eva. That's how it was. There was no deadlock, or even any question. I made the obvious decision that she would have the final say.

We had many discussions about how to do it, but in this case, she was the decision-maker and had the last word. This is called delegation.

After all, she was the expert and the expert should make the decisions.

TIME TO COMPROMISE?

We had something come up in our family that required many conferences between us. The children tossed in their opinions, too.

It had to do with buying a new couch. The one we had was an unsightly piece of furniture. Really broken down.

Although we had little money to spare, we did have just enough for a new couch. Eva and I were ready to pick one up, when a complication arose.

School let out for the year, and the children, who ranged in age from ten to fourteen, wanted to accompany me on a speaking trip a month later to Boston.

Only one catch. We didn't have enough money to go to Boston as a family and still buy a couch. It was one or the other. Which to do?

We batted it around for a few weeks. I discussed it with Eva. Eva discussed it with the children. I discussed it with the children. We all discussed it together at meals.

Either way, the family would have to do without something. A couch or a trip. It was a tough decision. I found myself on both sides of the question. So did Eva — and the children.

We kept tabling the matter. Finally, there were only a few days left before we would have to leave on the trip.

One point kept coming up in all the discussions.

"Dad, I sort of like our couch . . . even though it is all beat up," one of the children would invariably say.

And it was true. Even the gang from church seemed to enjoy the old couch. They would come in and throw their bodies into its beat-up frame without any reservation or worry of further damage.

"Well, I guess we've done OK with this couch up to this moment. Another year won't hurt us."

With that comment I decided to take the family with me to Boston.

We came home, happy with the trip, but still facing a decrepit, old couch. During the next year, all of us at one time or another wondered if we had made the right decision.

The couch was so bad that when we replaced it a year later, we called Goodwill Industries to come and take it away. And, you know, they turned it down.

We had to take it to the dump ourselves.

Some seemingly easy decisions can become complicated. There are no clear-cut solutions. But when the decisions are made, the issues are settled. You go on from there.

BOTH BACK UP THE DECISION!

Whichever of the two ways the husband settles the deadlock (his decision . . . delegating it), at that point both submit to the decision and do all in their power to make it work.

Let's summarize.

The second key is submission.

> Wives, be subject to your own husbands as to the Lord (Eph. 5:22).

It is the husband's duty to see to it that objectives, policies, procedures and rules are set up and carried out. Obviously, he would look to his wife to make decisions where she is best qualified. In deadlocks, he decides who settles it.

Coming to agreements doesn't necessarily guarantee they will be followed. That's the subject of our next chapter.

9 / Commitment: The Third Key (The Husband As Servant)

9 / Commitment: The Third Key (The Husband As Servant)

COMMITMENT: THE THIRD KEY

So the husband has the last word. He can break those unresolved deadlocks. And should. It's a biblical commandment, although being the head is much more than being "the boss."

> For the husband is the head of the wife, as Christ also is the head of the church, He Himself being the Savior of the body (Eph. 5:23).

What did Christ have to do? What was His mission to the church? He described it this way:

> For I did not speak on My own initiative, but the Father Himself who sent Me has given Me commandment, what to say, and what to speak. And I know that His commandment is eternal life; therefore the things I speak, I speak just as the Father has told Me (John 12:49,50).

Jesus was bound by His Father's words. What His Father had "commanded" leads us to eternal life. You can't beat instructions like those.

Heading a marriage means coming up with commandments (objectives, policies, rules) that lead to the eternal life of the marriage. Is this too idealistic? I think not.

A man and woman earnestly search the Bible for guidelines and diligently develop a working plan so the marriage will last until "death do us part." The husband leads the way in doing this and making the marriage better.

WHAT JESUS DID AS THE HEAD

Jesus had commandments from God that would lead us to eternal life. The Gospels show how He went about getting these commandments across to the people. He . . .

* taught	* lectured	* dealt with burdens
* discussed	* warned	and sickness
* reasoned	* overruled	* resisted injustice
* meditated	* rebuked	* expected loyalty
* suffered aggression		* moved aggressively
* dealt with challenges to His authority		

But he never changed the commands/rules.

HOW PEOPLE RESPONDED . . .

The people responded by . . . following, obeying, worshiping, being astonished and angry, arguing, resisting, betraying, and abandoning Him. It is said of Jesus:

He came to His own, and those who were His own did not receive Him (John 1:11).

But God demonstrates His own love toward us, in that while we were yet sinners, Christ died for us (Rom. 5:8).

Notice, the people are rejecting a man promising eternal life. Yet Jesus devoted His life to the church, even though many refused to follow Him.

It is my observation that we resist any rule, however beneficial, that gets in our way. The drive "to go our own way" isn't corrected by a set of rules. Not even if someone dies to defend them, as Jesus did.

THE PRICE OF HEADSHIP

If a husband's responsibility to his wife is the same as Christ's to the church, he must:

1. Take the lead in determining "commandments" that assure the eternal life of the marriage.

2. Work at carrying them out until death, whatever the resistance.

MARRIAGE — A FORTY-YEAR HAUL

This is what Jesus said about leadership:

Whoever wishes to be first among you shall be slave of all (Mark 10:44).

What then is expected of the husband? He is to be a lifetime slave to the task of making the marriage work.

Many a man gets a cold shoulder when he comes home. He can't count on his wife to carry out the rules. You might say she "sins" against the marriage. Still, he hangs in there until he dies.

Granted, men "sin" against the marriage, too. Leaders often do a lousy job. In that case, the wife hangs in for a lifetime.

You don't dump a business because you made some bad decisions. It may take a few years of blood, sweat, and tears to correct mistakes.

Marriage is a forty-year haul. There may be some bad years. You may even pile poor decision upon poor decision. But you stick it out.

How is this possible?

Only if God's love bathes your heart. Marriage is more than ceremony. It is hard work, sacrifice, and effort as you yield yourself to God's love. Because you yield yourself to God's love doesn't mean your partner will do so. To yield to God is a personal choice for each partner.

WHEN YOU MAKE A BAD DECISION

Most marriages have their sore spots. I think of a couple who bought a home far beyond their means. The husband yielded to his wife's pressure to buy it after resisting her for several years. Both soon agreed it was a mistake. Prices dropped, so they were stuck with it.

A bad decision. But both partners are working shoulder to shoulder to make the best of it. It may take years to get out from under this burden. No use jumping on her. The husband made the final decision. They were both wrong.

Another couple bought a house beyond their means. In this case, the husband purchased it in spite of his wife's protests. He told her he was the head of the house, and she was out of line sticking her nose into his business. She had no choice but to concede.

The decision was a bad one. His hopes for making large sums of money didn't materialize. Now they've got a heavy burden she didn't want in the first place. She was right. He was wrong. But they are working shoulder to shoulder to make the best of it.

We see another couple — in their early twenties, married three years. She has never learned to cook or keep house. To this day, their house is a shambles. At mealtime, they either eat out or each free-lances something out of the refrigerator. Neither knows any better. They live like two sloppy roommates. Tensions are growing between them.

Under these conditions, he is still the head. He needs to be coached step by step like the man-child he is. He gets no cooperation from his wife. The marriage is dying, but it doesn't have to. He can and is hanging in there, learning about the Christian life and leadership as fast as he can.

With patience, endurance, and hard work, he may yet save his marriage. He is staking his life on it. Is his wife persuaded to change because he is working on becoming a better leader? Not yet.

BLUEPRINT FROM GOD

Husbands do have some "orders" on what their attitudes toward their wives should be:

> For the husband is the head of the wife, as Christ also is the head of the church, He Himself being the Savior of the body. But as the church is subject to Christ, so also the wives ought to be to their husbands in everything. Husbands, love your wives, just as Christ also loved the church and gave Himself up for her; that He might sanctify her, having cleansed her by the washing of water with the word, that He might present to Himself the church in all her glory, having no spot or wrinkle or any such thing; but that she should be holy and blameless. So husbands ought to love their own wives as their own bodies. He who loves his own wife loves himself; for no one ever hated his own flesh, but nourishes and cherishes it, just as Christ also does the church, because we are members of His body. For this cause a man shall leave his father and

mother, and shall cleave to his wife; and the two shall become one flesh. This mystery is great; but I am speaking with reference to Christ and the church. Nevertheless let each individual among you also love his own wife even as himself; and let the wife see to it that she respect her husband (Eph. 5:23-33).

Let's examine a few high spots of these verses.

A LOVE THAT WON'T QUIT

Husbands, love your wives, just as Christ also loved the church and gave Himself up for her (Eph. 5:25).

Your wife can't stop you from loving her — if you draw your love from God. The kind of love is described in chapter 5 of this book and is based on 1 Corinthians 13:4-8. Love:

* is patient	* rejoices not in unrighteousness
* is kind	* rejoices with the truth
* is not jealous	* bears all things
* does not brag	* believes all things
* is not arrogant	* hopes all things
* does not act unbecoming	* endures all things
* doesn't seek its own way	* never fails
* is not provoked easily	* doesn't take into account a wrong suffered

Your love for your wife has nothing to do with her choices. Your love involves yielding yourself to God.

. . . The love of God has been poured out within our hearts through the Holy Spirit who was given to us (Rom. 5:5).

A GOAL THAT WON'T QUIT

That He might present to Himself the church in all her glory, having no spot or wrinkle or any such thing; but that she should be holy and blameless (Eph. 5:27).

This verse implies that you keep trying to help your wife become the finest person possible. If she rejects your efforts, back off for a while — even for a few years. Here is more advice to husbands:

You husbands likewise, live with your wives in an understanding way, as with a weaker vessel, since she is a woman, and grant her honor as a fellow-heir of the grace of life, so that your prayers may not be hindered. To sum up, let all be

> harmonious, sympathetic, brotherly, kind-hearted, and humble in spirit; not returning evil for evil, or insult for insult, but giving a blessing instead; for you were called for the very purpose that you might inherit a blessing. For "let him who means to love life and see good days refrain his tongue from evil and his lips from speaking guile" (1 Peter 3:7-10).

Yes, let the husband get to know his wife, honor her, and treat her as he would a rare, precious, delicate vase. *Even if she tells him to get lost.*

Jesus gives some advice and tacks a promise onto it:

> And just as you want men to treat you, treat them in the same way. And if you love those who love you, what credit is that to you? For even sinners love those who love them. And if you do good to those who do good to you, what credit is that to you? For even sinners do the same thing. And if you lend to those from whom you expect to receive, what credit is that to you? Even sinners lend to sinners, in order to receive back the same amount. But love your enemies, and do good, and lend, expecting nothing in return; and your reward will be great, and you will be sons of the Most High; for He Himself is kind to ungrateful and evil men. Be merciful, just as your Father is merciful. And do not pass judgment and you will not be judged; and do not condemn, and you shall not be condemned; pardon, and you will be pardoned. Give, and it will be given to you; good measure, pressed down, shaken together, running over, they will pour into your lap. For whatever measure you deal out to others, it will be dealt to you in return (Luke 6:31-38).

Seldom does a family break up if the husband is truly loving and diligently searches out ways to help his wife become the finest person she could possibly be.

Usually it's the other way around. The husband is bitter, hostile, and has quit trying. He is preoccupied with himself and filled with self-pity. He thinks about getting even, rather than healing the marriage. These attitudes cause marriages to collapse.

How long do you endure?

Until death.

That's what Jesus did.

LOVE HER AS YOU LOVE YOURSELF

So husbands ought also to love their own wives as their own

bodies. He who loves his own wife loves himself (Eph. 5:28).

I once had an experience that showed me how much I loved my own body. I dropped something on my little toe, which, until then, I had hardly noticed.

Suddenly, my toe was the center of attraction. I bathed, wrapped, favored it, even changed my way of walking for the sake of that toe.

When your body is healthy, you are hardly aware of its parts. Let one part get hurt, and it demands your attention.

Your marriage is like that. Without conflicts, you are hardly aware of attitudes or rules. When there is a conflict, it demands your attention.

When your wife is hurting, when there is strain or tension, it is a signal for your individual attention. You take the initiative. This is no simple matter if your efforts are resisted.

Your wife is entitled to this kind of dedication. She can call problems to your attention, can express her views, make recommendations and have them taken seriously. She has half interest in this partnership. You have left father and mother and have become one. Your goal is to become so committed to each other that you respond as one person, rather than two.

THE HUSBAND'S TOP PRIORITY

If I understand the Bible, the husband's top priority is his wife. Not his work. Not his recreation. Not the children.

But . . . his wife.

If a husband understands this, he tries to use all the talent and ability of both partners.

He is responsible for harmonious relationships. He has enough meetings with his wife to make sure the duties of the partnership are carried out. This takes his best daily and weekly efforts "until death do us part."

That's some assignment. The divorce rate would drop dramatically if we men held up our end of our marriage.

SOUND A LITTLE BETTER?

How's that, ladies? This is God's plan for managing a marriage. Sound a little better now?

There is submission on the part of both parties.

First, husband and wife agree to develop and maintain a plan which both will support.

Second, the wife submits to her husband's judgment when there is a deadlock.

Third, the husband submits to the responsibility of making the plan work.

That's leadership.

'Til death do us part.

10 / Handling the Routines

10 / Handling the Routines

EVERYONE HAS TO WORK THESE OUT . . .

Everyone has routines — regular, unvarying procedures repeated over and over, day after day. A newly married couple must develop routines for living together.

Remember Ken and Nancy? They clashed over how fast to drive, driving style, eating style, and neatness — all on their first day. The problems wouldn't go away. They had to be resolved.

Everyone has to face routines. Doctor, dentist, lawyer, counselor . . . all face a daily schedule, office procedures, handling money, filling out forms — routines.

Even if you live alone, you face routines.

We know a single woman whose day demands that she pay attention to a multitude of details.

To start, she must get out of bed. This implies owning a bed, bed sheets, pillows, pillowcases, and blankets. It means changing sheets, washing and storing all these articles. It also means having paid for, or being in the process of paying for, these items.

Preparation for going to work means some bathroom equipment — soap, deodorants, perfumes, curlers, scissors, towels. Then there is clothing, which means more purchasing, cleaning, pressing, washing, storing, replacing, and adding.

Eating breakfast requires purchasing, storing, cooking, dishes, utensils, silverware, washing. It also involves scheduling time.

Then off to work, which requires financing and maintaining a car, garage, and driveway.

Her job requires purchasing and maintaining some equipment, some study, getting along with others.

After work, she likes to relax in her living room. This means furniture, rugs, drapes, curtains, a TV, a radio, a newspaper. It involves cleaning house, washing windows, furnishing heat.

The house sits on a lot, which involves cutting grass, working on flower beds.

Then there is the evening. This may mean sports, restaurants, church, parties at her house or someone else's, more clothes and equipment.

Then it's bedtime, and setting an alarm.

There are extras like unexpected company, a leaky roof, light bulbs, sickness, a leaky hot-water heater which ruined the linoleum, or going on a trip.

This isn't a complete list. A little thought could double it. If you make a list, you'll get a visual picture of your routines.

When you marry, your partner may have a list of daily routines that matches yours item for item. Even then, you may differ from one another in the way you carry them out. If so, your two plans for the day will collide.

THE HUSBAND'S FIRST ASSIGNMENT

The process of defining and redefining similarities and differences in handling routines begins before marriage and continues as long as you live.

The husband takes the lead, examining routines that need attention.

It is a very long list.

So you begin. Two children of God, with His love in your hearts — cooperative, submissive, committed. Without His love, your efforts will deadlock again and again.

Does this frighten you? Well, it should jolt you into

recognizing that launching and maintaining a marriage is not just a ceremony. <u>You must each carefully study your living patterns.</u>

Blending routines (or becoming "one flesh," as the Bible puts it) requires a good deal of study, trial and error, give and take. It won't be done in a month, or even two. You will have many discussions and decisions to face.

Get the picture?

<u>Launching a marriage is easy.</u>

<u>Keeping it going requires the same time, attention, and effort as a business partnership. And I mean *daily* effort.</u>

MOVE SLOWLY

Agreeing on how to handle the routines of your marriage boils down to agreeing on policies, procedures, rules, and assignments.

One caution: limit your discussions to an hour or less. You can't handle everything in a day. Some issues may have to wait until next week before you can even bring them up.

After a while, you will discover that some of your initial procedures and rules aren't really satisfactory. They need to be revised.

After a year or two, you no longer deal with first-time decisions. New ones surface continually. Also, old ones need to be changed.

DECISION-MAKING REVEALS YOUR SPIRIT

Marvin and Gail brought a collection of unresolved issues to the consulting room. One involved some odd contrasts.

Marvin required a tablecloth for all meals, including breakfast. Gail considered this totally unreasonable.

He had another habit that drove Gail up the wall. You see, Gail was taught to ask for things rather than reach. Not Marvin. He would reach across the table, stab at the sugar bowl, come up with a heaping spoonful but leave a trail of sugar from the bowl to his cup. That trail burned Gail up.

Neither Marvin nor Gail conceded on this simple

issue. Instead of settling the issue, they revealed a mutual stubbornness that needed to be dealt with before the issue could be settled. Love doesn't seek its own way.

EATING

Nora dreads having company for dinner because of her husband's eating habits. He takes portions of everything — meat, potatoes, vegetables — and ritualistically mixes them together in a pile. This embarrasses Nora, but he refuses to change.

She fights back — thus there are two stubborn wills. There is no repentance, so the deadlock over eating habits perpetuates.

If both husband and wife cooperate, they can enjoy buying food, cooking, serving, adjusting timing of meals, establishing eating habits, and cleaning up afterward. Without this attitude, routines become a lifetime battleground. We throw all theories about cooperation and submission out the window and "go our own way."

HELPING

A minister noticed one Monday — his day off — that his wife was swamped that day with washing and getting the noon lunch ready for their three children. He relieved her by preparing the lunch himself. She was delighted. Soon, every Monday his "surprise" lunch was one of the highlights of the week.

Another couple solved the bed-making problem. The last one up does it — before that person leaves the bedroom. This way, a mutually disagreeable job got passed around.

Washing dishes isn't the greatest job. So, one husband dried the dishes after the Sunday dinner while his wife washed them. He helped her and kept her company — instead of racing off to the ball game on television.

CLEANING

A friend of mine and his wife were visiting some acquaintances, when his wife casually acknowledged their sparkling kitchen floor.

116

"Thanks . . . that's my husband's job, though. He gets the credit," the lady of the house replied.

Her husband was in charge of all the floors. He also washed the windows. My friend was flabbergasted. Imagine a man doing those things.

Any arrangement you two agree on between yourselves is your affair. It's your partnership.

STRATEGY FOR AN EVENING

How do you handle the evening?

The husband comes home. He has worked a long, full day. So has the wife, even though she's been home all day.

Both are probably tired. Yet, as partners, they must decide how to have a good supper, a time of fun with the children afterward, and then make sure everyone gets to bed on time.

You tailor a plan that fits both of you. Maybe mom does everything one night — dad the next. Some couples split the responsibilities nightly. Still others give the job to one partner or the other as a full-time responsibility.

If your plan for handling the evening isn't clear, you need a conference.

TUESDAY IS MY NIGHT . . .

"I never get to watch my Tuesday night program," Joan lamented to her husband. That's all Peter needed. They discussed it and decreed:

From then on, Peter took most of the responsibility on Tuesday night. That way, his wife was able to get her business out of the way by 9 o'clock. She got to watch her program once a week.

That's not too much to ask — or is it? It was their partnership.

"I'M WIPED OUT . . ."

Some night, one of you might be wiped out.

"Could you take over my responsibilities, honey?" should be a request taken seriously by a partner committed to adjusting with the best interests of the couple in mind.

"MARTHA, WHERE'S THE SPORTS SECTION?"

George and Martha have a running debate about the daily newspaper. He insists it should be kept neatly together. She likes to catch a little reading on the side. As a result, one section ends up in the bedroom, another in the bathroom, one in the living room, still another in the kitchen. On occasion, George hunts around for a paper, then yells:

"Martha, where's the sports section?"

A few minutes later they track it down — wrapped around the garbage.

This newspaper issue is such a continuous battle, it should become an item for discussion — and be settled.

OFF TO DETROIT . . .

Handling daily routines often produces unexpected surprises. When Eva and I travel, I usually drive and she watches the map. Sounds good, doesn't it?

I was in for one of those surprises one day when Eva and I were between family life conferences. I had just finished teaching married couples how to get along. I was the expert. All had thanked me for helping them.

Enroute to the next conference we stopped at a motel. I like to go first class, so we chose the finest motel and slept on the best mattress money could buy.

In the morning, we bathed, applied appropriate deodorants and perfumes the ads tell us to, ate a good breakfast, and started out in our big, air-conditioned Olds 98.

When you are clean, properly scented, well fed, well dressed, in a big new car and surrounded by gorgeous scenery, you should have it made.

All went well until we came to two intersecting freeways. One led to Detroit. The other to Chicago. We turned onto the freeway headed for Detroit. Eva, the navigator, piped up.

"Henry, you turned the wrong way."

Instantly, I was furious and shouted at her:

"Eva, for goodness sake, don't you think I know

where Detroit is? I grew up in this state! Do you want to drive this car?"

Having your wife put you down like that is enough to make anyone mad. Right? Surely, God's love isn't available to a man at a time like this, is it?

Mind you, all she was doing was acting as the navigator — doing her job (handling routines reveals your spirit).

I accelerated angrily and glared at the road ahead. Eva didn't say a word. Silence filled the car as we sped along.

Then we came to a highway sign by an exit.

There was an arrow pointing in the direction we were going. And above the arrow it said:

"Chicago."

I am a Ph.D. I am skilled at evaluating data and making accurate judgments from it. Yet, I completely ignored that sign — and away we went.

We came to another exit sign. It said the same thing. I found myself becoming more angry at Eva.

Can you believe it? Notice the limitations of education, good housing, cleanliness, money. In spite of all these, in a fit of temper, I was acting like a stupid fool.

Still, I decided to try one more sign. Eva didn't say a thing. Nor did she comment when we came to the next sign which again said: "Chicago." This was the third exit down the pike. We were headed west — not east. I knew that.

Yet, my mind was working as fast as it could go. Guess what I was thinking? Right. *I wonder how I can get to Detroit without turning around.*

How do you get turned around when you are wrong, know it, yet won't admit it? At that moment, you couldn't have dragged me off that freeway.

There is a way. The Bible says:

> If we confess our sins, He is faithful and righteous to forgive us our sins and to cleanse us from all unrighteousness (1 John 1:9).

Sounds easy. What were my sins? I've asked this

question of many audiences, and their response is so immediate and complete that at times I've had to cut them off.

Pride . . . rebellion . . . anger . . . stubbornness. These are just a few they suggest. It's easy to identify our sins if we want to.

I didn't want to face the truth. It was a struggle.

Finally, I told God I was sorry. Would He forgive me? Would He renew His love in my heart? Of course He would. My attitude changed immediately. I told Eva:

"I think I'm headed in the wrong direction."

I began looking eagerly for the next exit so we could get going toward Detroit.

DECISIONS CAN WAIT

If this stubborn spirit emerges in your discussion, drop the matter until you or your partner repents. It may take thirty seconds . . . a day . . . a month. Whenever, talk to God as His child. He will forgive and bathe your heart with His love.

Then get on with the business of settling issues and handling never-ending routines.

✳ A LIFE-CHANGING CONCEPT ✳

Your serenity, peace, joy, and love are not determined by your partner's choices. Your inner condition is *revealed,* not created, by your partner's choices.

Routines will reveal your spirit. Whether or not you let God bathe your heart with His love is your choice. Your partner can't stop you — no matter how nasty or inconsiderate he or she is. (This is a good time to review chapter 5 of this book and refresh your memory on what God's love is.)

START WITH FAITH

God's love will help you effectively handle the routines of married life.

Remember: *marriage involves dealing with a multitude of details on a daily basis.*

It takes faith to entrust the deadlocks to your husband's or your wife's judgment. It takes faith from both partners for the husband to make decisions in the best interests of the family, especially when the wife is convinced her judgment should prevail.

Can we say it too many times?

Only God's love in both partners will make harmony possible as you handle the routines.

11 / Sex . . . Money . . . Change

11 / Sex . . . Money . . . Change

WHAT'S THE PROBLEM?

Everyone enjoys looking at and touching the human body. Advertisers know a pretty woman or virile man will catch our eye — and our emotions.

Remember your dating days? A thrilling response to your date was as automatic as responding to the aroma of good food or fine perfume. You had no serious problem figuring out how to touch, hug, caress, or kiss. Your problem was restraining yourself.

Isn't it strange, then, that so many married people struggle with sexual relations when touching, caressing, kissing, and coitus are the most ecstatic experiences in life — enjoyed by both men and women?

**THE MOST COMMON TROUBLE
SPOT — SEXUAL RELATIONS**

Almost every married couple who comes to my consulting room presents their sex life as a major problem. But never is this the only issue.

A beautiful, shapely lady came, bruised and battered by her husband. They had these slugfests frequently. She usually started them with angry tirades because he came home late or wrote checks without telling her.

When there was no conflict, they had a beautiful

sex life. Attitudes toward sex, technique, frequency, or position weren't issues. When there was conflict, fistfights replaced tenderness and sexual activity.

This couple illustrates the fallacy that sexual satisfaction enables two people to get along better.

We've all read books and articles that blame present sexual difficulties on parents, early teachings about sex, early experiences with sex, lack of knowledge about how the body is made, about positions and techniques.

Not so.

People who *want* to respond sexually will find a way. Information is easily available if it is needed or wanted.

Consider a baby. What determines whether a baby is cuddled, kissed, spoken to with endearing words — or ignored, spanked, and yelled at?

In either case, it's the same baby. Yet the parent's response depends on whether the baby is laughing or crying, is digesting its food or throwing it up, has a clean or dirty diaper, is behaving or misbehaving. Then, too, it depends on whether the parent is patient or impatient, angry or happy, self-seeking or serving.

Is your response to your partner not the same as to a baby? What's simpler than touching your partner, caressing, kissing, speaking endearing words?

What causes you to pull away, stiffen up, resist? Surely it's not a question of enjoyment. Everyone enjoys some kind of physical contact.

What determines whether you caress or slap? Speak tenderly or harshly? The same beautiful bodies are involved.

The biblical standard for expressing yourselves sexually is *total freedom and equality between husband and wife.*

> Let the husband fulfill his duty to his wife, and likewise also the wife to her husband. The wife does not have authority over her own body, but the husband does; and likewise also the husband does not have authority over his own body, but the wife does. Stop depriving one another, except by agreement for a time that you may devote yourselves to prayer, and come together again lest Satan tempt you because of your lack of self-control (1 Cor. 7:3-5).

In other words, *your partner's wish is your command*. Wow! You didn't expect such freedom in marriage. Right?

KNOW YOUR PARTNER

General information about what "men" or "women" are like won't serve you here. You must know your partner's needs, likes, dislikes to find a mutually agreeable way to express your sexual wishes. It is God's love in your heart that will serve you . . . love that:

. . . does not act unbecoming	. . . does not seek its own
	. . . does not take into
. . . does not provoke	account a wrong suffered

The *big three* become important here:

1. Cooperation
2. Submission
3. Commitment

If the Bible clearly describes *total sexual freedom* and *equality* between husband and wife, what is it, then, that determines whether you turn your faces or backs to each other?

SELF-SEEKING

As I have listened to people talk about the struggle with their physical response to one another, self-seeking usually comes up as a problem. There are *deadlocks* over money, housing, social life, church life, family life, in-laws, use of time, most anything. It is not surprising that they would be deadlocked over meeting each other's sexual wishes.

DEEDS OF THE FLESH

Also, there are deeds of the flesh. Unresolved issues between partners reveal reactions of anger, hatred, bitterness, rebellion. With such reactions, sacrificing sexual satisfaction seems more desirable than pleasing a partner.

By now, we know how to handle self-seeking and deeds of the flesh. This is a personal matter between you and God. Repent, ask God to cleanse you, and once more bathe your heart with His love.

What if your partner doesn't repent? Or cooperate? You don't deprive your partner. There is a warning contained in 1 Corinthians 7:5:

> Stop depriving one another, except by agreement for a time that you may devote yourselves to prayer, and come together again lest Satan tempt you because of your lack of self-control.

The only reason for depriving your partner is to devote yourselves to long periods of prayer and fasting. That doesn't happen very often. Otherwise, if you deprive one another, you can be tempted seriously.

"THERE'S SOMEONE ELSE . . . "

"I'm married and attracted to another person to whom I'm not married."

This is a comment I hear with increasing frequency coming from both men and women, Christian and non-Christian.

I've had individuals who can't stand the sight of their married partner — much less respond physically — describe a torrid physical affair with someone else (sometimes even a stranger) who is not nearly as attractive or personable as the marriage partner. The new involvement is simply an expression of resentment or retaliation. Surely it is not an expression of the love of God.

Physical response is obviously not the problem. It's a matter of the spirit . . . a matter of the will, not the body.

Granted, there are temptations everywhere. When haven't there been?

After all, half the people in the world are women, roughly speaking. That's about two billion women. The other half of the people are men. When you become a wife, all the men out there don't disappear. Nor do the women disappear when a man gets married. They are there . . . and are still interesting and attractive.

Beautiful women and virile men were God's idea, you know. You can enjoy the beauty and fellowship of both sexes without lusting after them. You can have many close friends of both sexes. Granted, these relationships sometimes are hard to handle.

A MATTER OF COMMITMENT

Marriage involves commitment to one person, even though other people are still there.

A child of God, with the love of God in his heart, who means to cooperate with his partner, who means to submit, and who proves it in other areas, won't have a sex problem — either with his partner, or with someone else. Note the conditions. Take the Bible seriously and you will be on your way to a beautiful sex life. You will want to please your partner.

What if your partner gives you a cold shoulder in spite of your willingness to follow the biblical command?

Stay available. Desire to do your part. Remember, these problems are not solved in a day, or even in a year. Your commitment is to God. Your commitment does not depend on your partner's choice. You stand by, yielding to the love of God. He will sustain you. Love endures. That's good news, not bad news. Try it.

MONEY PROBLEMS

Yes, sex is the struggle people discuss the most in the consulting room. But in strong second place is the struggle over money.

I have had to help hundreds of my clients work their way out of financial trouble.

Here is my homespun advice.

No one has trouble spending money. The challenge is how to keep some of it. Anyone who has some money has obviously not spent all of it.

People in financial trouble have spent more than they have made. Sound elementary? Yes. But to ignore this simple fact is to get into trouble.

Where do you begin if you are in trouble? First, draw up a financial statement of your assets and liabilities. If you don't understand what I mean, then seek out someone to help you. Now you must face your creditors.

Second, if bill collectors are hounding you, go to each person to whom you owe money and frankly discuss your situation. Then work out a pay-back agreement with them. You may need to turn to someone who has experience in handling money. This may be a humiliating experience, but it is the first step upward. You should do this whether you draw a welfare check, an unemployment check, or make $25,000 a year.

Next, plan to live within your income. Here, again, you may need some counsel.

The important step is *the will to do it.* This may mean some drastic changes in your life style.

MY STORY

Let me share with you a bit of my own story about finances.

I will be eternally grateful to an inexperienced Christian education director and a Sunday school teacher for their help.

First, the Christian education director. He was always asking me what I was doing with my money. I figured it was none of his business. But he kept it up anyway.

He kept rubbing my nose in two Bible verses:

> But seek first His kingdom and His righteousness; and all these things shall be added to you.
>
> Therefore do not be anxious for tomorrow; for tomorrow will care for itself. Each day has enough trouble of its own (Matt. 6:33,34).

After months of trying to push these words of Jesus out of my mind and avoiding that minister, I finally gave in. I got out a pencil and sketched out the use of my time and money.

After I did my work, looked after the yard, played tennis, went sailing, my week was up. I spent very little time at home. All my money was spent on me and mine. My life was the reverse of what Jesus taught in those verses.

I promised Jesus I would obey His commandment to "seek first His kingdom."

This was a new way of life. Gradually, I developed a new set of priorities. Here they are:

1. Wife
2. Children
3. Ministry
4. Making a living

Such priorities required a drastic change in my life style. My emphasis changed from money, money, money, to thinking about my family and service to people. This emphasis drew me into the church, and eventually into changing from engineering to counseling and teaching. This gradual change began when I was 27 and continues to this day.

We developed a new financial plan also. Whatever income came along, big or small, we divided it as follows:

1. Tithe...10%
2. Living expenses/savings..........85%
3. Risk money 5%

I couldn't imagine how I could give away ten percent of my income as a tithe, but we decided to do it. This has been one of the best financial decisions I have ever made.

THE RISK MONEY WAS THE KEY . . .

Why five percent for risk money? The idea was planted in my mind by a beloved Sunday school teacher, a very wealthy man.

I was working on my Ph.D. degree at Cornell University at the time. I decided to study full time, so I asked this man to lend me the money to do it.

He did — but added a little speech:

"Henry, I am lending you this money to show you I believe in you and to encourage you. This is like lending you one of my finest tools.

"This is part of my 'risk money.' You see, I use money to make money. When I lend it to you, I can't use it. I'm investing in you."

Wow! I heard this speech and made two commitments as a result:

1. I would see to it that his investment in me paid off.

2. I would also build up some "risk money."

So that's how rich people do it. If you want to have money, you can't spend it all. I vowed to set aside five percent of my income as investment money like the rich people.

This fund accumulated slowly at first, but I kept looking for an investment. Across the years, the Lord has given me wisdom far beyond myself for handling that money. Starting from zero, that money has been multiplied hundreds of times, and has made it possible for me to give many thousands of dollars back to the Lord's work.

I'll spare you the details but leave you with the principle once more: if you tithe and put aside some risk money (assuming you seek first His kingdom and righteousness) God gives you the wisdom to multiply it.

How do I know? Because I've been privileged to help many people straighten out their tangled financial affairs, establish priorities, and get on their feet spiritually and financially.

You and your partner must determine your percentages between you and the Lord.

There are books in any library that will counsel you as to your financial problems. Many banks and lending institutions also provide materials on handling money.

As I said at the beginning, this book isn't a detailed financial guide. My purpose is to challenge you to learn how to multiply your money to the glory of our Lord and get your priorities in order.

FACING CHANGE — A COMMON PROBLEM

One of the toughest adjustments a marriage faces is sudden change. There are job changes or losses. There are moves. Unexpected pregnancies. Sicknesses. Broken bones. Financial reverses. Financial gains. The children grow up through various stages. They leave to launch their own careers. How well you meet the changes depends on how committed you are to your God and your partner.

JACK AND JAN WENT UP . . .

Jack and Jan went up the hill of a drastic kind of change. Jack was firmly settled in a demanding job in a big city. Every evening he came home from the day's pressures and the rush of commuting, and collapsed into his easy chair.

But not for long. Their evenings were full.

Jack joined Jan in volunteer work at the local YMCA. Along with their two children, they went to other evening attractions or participated in family-centered activities. For nearly fifteen years, this was their pattern.

Then, one day, Jan dropped a bombshell.

What would Jack think if she became a lawyer? It sounded like a joke at first, but the more they discussed it, the more obvious it became that Jan was serious. With the children in school, she needed a challenge.

Together, they started figuring what would be involved. The next five years would be spent in schooling and apprenticeship-type work. It would be quite an undertaking.

But they decided to do it.

That was two years ago. One Saturday afternoon I was at the grocery store and ran into Jack doing the shopping for the family.

"Not watching the ball game this afternoon?"

"No," said Jack. "Don't see many ball games any more." But then he quickly added:

"You know, I haven't minded it that much. I come home from work, and there is Jan studying her heart out. She's doing well, getting all B-plusses and A's. I think _we're_ going to make it."

Well said, I thought. It is a _"we"_ thing, this matter of handling changes of all sorts in the home.

You may ask how this will turn out. We don't know. His commitment has to continue, as does hers. And if she gets her law degree, there will be more changes. Their commitment to each other, and their style of living, will be in for many reviews.

JEANETTE MARRIED A PASTOR . . .

I observed a beautiful happening that was mixed with sadness, but it illustrates how a family can be forced to face uncontrollable and sudden change.

Jeanette was a superb organist and pianist. She did the obvious and married a pastor. You can imagine what a helper she was, for she was also a warm, loving person and

133

helped many of the women of the church.

They had two children. Jeanette and her husband were delighted with their family life and ministry.

Then Jeanette was stricken with polio. Almost overnight, this highly talented, busy woman was an invalid.

The routines went out the window. Her husband, in addition to his duties as a pastor, had to nurse an invalid wife, get the washing and ironing done, get the children off to school, do the shopping and housecleaning.

Over the months, Jeanette fought back — from the bed to the wheelchair. Then, gradually, she started taking back her duties around the house. She even made it back to that organ in spite of her crippled condition.

Through the entire ordeal, the two of them maintained a cheery spirit as they let the love of God bathe their hearts.

This "for better or worse" story shows how partners move along day by day, by faith, and discover their marriage growing stronger.

A PROBLEM FOR THE NEWLYWEDS

They were only eighteen when they married. They had their goals. He would go to college full time and she would work. They bought a trailer and had it hauled up to the college trailer park. What a cozy love nest! How happy they were!

But they were a glum-looking couple the day they came to my office.

She got pregnant shortly after their marriage. He blamed her, and she blamed him. Neither had anticipated this possibility. He was so disturbed, he dropped out of college.

And she was very sick — and big.

There was only hate between them.

"The pregnancy caused it," he said. "It's all her fault."

No. Pregnancy revealed the hatred. These two didn't invent unexpected pregnancies. Multitudes of couples have had the same experience and survived quite well.

I taught them how to repent of their hatred for each other, be cleansed, and find God's love. This unexpected change turned out to be the opposite of tragedy. It introduced them to God.

That's good.

They quit fighting and started cooperating. They developed a new plan for their lives. All was well — and still is.

FOR THREE YEARS . . . THE POORHOUSE!

Calvin and Liz were broke all the time because Cal was going to medical school. He barely had time for any part-time jobs, and Liz worked full time, teaching third grade at an elementary school near their mobile home.

There was never any money left over. It all went for school expenses and the minuscule budget they had set up.

But they were happy. They were dedicated to one goal: getting Cal that title of M.D. Liz took her hard schedule without complaint. Cal helped whenever he could and made sure he kept his grades up.

Together, they reached their goal.

It was a tough grind. They literally had been in the poorhouse. Just the basics in food and seldom any new clothes. Somehow, they enjoyed it.

Cal joined two other doctors in a successful private practice. In a year, Cal became a full partner. Only twelve months away from poverty, Cal and Liz were approaching prosperity.

Calvin's job fascinated him. He worked long and hard — but satisfying — hours. Soon, they had retired their past debts. Now, he and Liz became fascinated with gadgets . . . boats and trailers . . . clubs . . . cottages . . . specialty foods . . . expensive restaurants . . . entertainment . . . whole wardrobes of new clothes.

Their social life turned them on as well. Cal headed up the cancer drive for a year. Liz was pushed to the head of the women's group. She was consumed with her new interest in the tennis club as well. Calvin was ape over golf.

Only a few years ago, they had been living in

poverty. Now Cal and Liz were completely caught up in these new, pleasant, challenging, fascinating experiences.

By now, a child was born . . . and being raised by baby sitters.

Gradually, it began to dawn on Cal and Liz that they were unhappy. They didn't see too much of each other any more. When they were together, there was more bickering than fellowship. The whole thing was confusing. Where did the teamwork and fellowship go that was so precious to them while Cal was in med school and Liz was helping him through?

Now, they were going separate but interesting ways. The marriage was suffering. They were playing singles again.

So they ended up in my consulting room. How come two brilliant, educated, talented people with ample money to spend end up like this? It seemed they had the world at their feet.

This is a common garden variety kind of problem, like the common cold. It's ageless. It was happening back in the apostle Paul's day. He wrote:

> I know how to get along with humble means, and I also know how to live in prosperity; in any and every circumstance I have learned the secret of being filled and going hungry, both of having abundance and suffering need (Phil. 4:12).

Cal and Liz had not learned this secret. He was trained in the medical profession, but didn't know how to handle prosperity.

Multitudes of Americans like Cal and Liz have not learned how to handle prosperity. Their prosperity brought out clearly in them the drive "to go your own way." Prosperity revealed a lack of the love of God. They learned that education, brilliance, and wealth are not substitutes for God's love.

WHAT WAS THE ANSWER?

1. Cal and Liz, intelligent, talented, prosperous, needed a Savior.

2. Through Jesus, they could let the love of God bathe their hearts.

3. They needed to submit themselves to each other.

4. Cal needed to take leadership in the home. He needed to look after his relationship to his wife as he did to his own body.

This was a stiff dose for Cal and Liz. They fought these steps for many months before realizing they couldn't do it on their own.

YOU CAN COUNT ON CHANGE

Changes will come. No one orders his own life to come out as he wants it to. It was Jesus who said:

> These things I have spoken to you, that in Me you may have peace. In the world you have tribulation, but take courage; I have overcome the world (John 16:33).

Read what the apostle Paul wrote:

> And we know that God causes all things to work together for good to those who love God, to those who are called according to His purpose (Rom. 8:28).

IT WILL BE GOOD . . .

Your partner going back to school to enter a profession? Polio? Unexpected pregnancy? Poorly handled prosperity?

How could these circumstances work together for good? But they did. No one understands the benefits of trials, difficulties, or conflicts as he goes through them. But for a child of God, with His love in your heart, it all adds up for good. As you look back, you see the benefits. As you go through the day, or peer out into the future, you trust God.

The child of God has a zest for life. So, bring on the future!

It will be good.

With God as your source, you can expect to respond to life as the apostle Paul describes it:

> Rejoice always; pray without ceasing; in everything give thanks; for this is God's will for you in Christ Jesus (1 Thess. 5:16-18).

12 / Let the Church Roll On . . . and Help Your Marriage

12 / Let the Church Roll On . . . and Help Your Marriage

THE MOST IMPORTANT CHAPTER?

This may be the most important chapter of the book.

Why?

If you want your marriage to be better, you must build it upon a spiritual foundation. Right? Your Christian education is basic to building that foundation.

Where do you turn for the help you need? *You turn to the church.*

UP WITH THE CHURCH!

I'm for the church and church-related groups. By the church, I refer to your local church, denominations, and church-related groups like Youth for Christ, Young Life, Navigators, Campus Crusade for Christ, Inter-Varsity, Christian Business Men's Committee, Christian camps and conferences, Christian radio and TV, Christian schools, Christian colleges, missionary organizations, et al.

They are the custodians of the most important information in the world — God's word to men and women.

These groups provided me with the information that led me into an abundant life through Jesus Christ. They handed me the keys to keeping my marriage intact and to raising my children. They taught me how to help other people.

They have even given me a platform from which to minister. I've cast my lot with the church.

To me, the hope for the mental health of the world rests in their hands. We can't lift ourselves by our own bootstraps. Only God has the power we need. The church points you Godward and teaches you how to avail yourself of His resources.

I know hundreds of couples who credit their church with providing the instruction, guidance, and fellowship that helped them sustain their marriages.

When people criticize Christians, I always ask: "Which Christian?"

Granted, any close look at all Christians would find them ranking from the best to the worst.

I have specialized in counseling Christians. I've seen their seamy side. But they don't contradict the Bible's teachings. They illustrate them. Who hasn't sometime fallen on his or her face? The Bible tells us why we fall, how to get up, and how to stand. The finest people I know are Christians. And, yes, some of the worst.

You don't write off Weight Watchers because someone followed their instructions, took off pounds, and then put them on again. No, you conclude they quit following instructions.

THE MINISTRY OF A SUNDAY SCHOOL TEACHER

I'll never forget a big, husky, powerful man who was very wealthy — and my Sunday school teacher. He didn't need to be my Sunday school teacher. He could have been concentrating on his investments. Or sitting in another Sunday school class, taking in Bible teaching for himself.

Instead, he taught a bunch of rebels.

Every week we planned our strategy with one goal: how to make life miserable for him.

Eventually, I turned completely away from him, the church, and Jesus Christ. I got involved in some wild living.

Yet, every time he'd see me, he would corner me. I hated to see him coming.

But come he would. Then, he would put that big,

powerful arm around me and take hold of my bony shoulder with his big hand.

"Henry, I love you, but I don't like what you're doing. You're doing wrong."

That burned me up. I'd mutter as he walked away, "Why doesn't he mind his own business?"

Later, he told me. He was minding his own business. He was my Sunday school teacher, so *I was his business.*

Even though I was mad at him, I admitted he was a man of good judgment. And he kept coming after me.

I'm glad today.

By the way, this is the same man who loaned me the money to finish my last year at the university.

A NURSE . . . PLUS THE CHURCH

A dentist friend of mine was separated from his wife. They couldn't stand each other.

The nurse in his office was a Christian and kept after him to go to a Billy Graham Crusade — which happened to be going on at that time in their city.

He resisted. Finally, so she'd stop pestering him, he went — but sat as far away from Dr. Graham as he could.

Yet, when the invitation was given, he found himself crawling out of the second balcony and walking down to accept Christ.

Shortly after that, he sought out his wife and pleaded with her to go with him to a weekend retreat at a conference center.

She was flabbergasted at the change in him. He'd been hard and tough but now was mild and tender. She was sure he had an ulterior motive.

But she went — and she, too, turned to Christ.

They were reunited.

Six months later, I was getting off a plane in San Francisco to go to a conference at this same retreat center. The dentist was there to meet me.

Holding onto one arm was his wife. Cradled in the other arm was my Moody Bible Institute correspondence course, *Keys to Better Living for Parents.*

143

Between the Billy Graham Crusade . . . the conference center . . . and my correspondence course on the home, his marriage had been saved. Attending a local church weekly, he learned how to live the Christian life. Today, he helps others.

THE MINISTRY OF A MINISTER

I will be eternally grateful to some ministers and missionaries who helped me along the way — those who kept asking me pesky questions like
* What do you do with your time?
* What do you do with your money?
* Are you happy?
* Are you neglecting your family?

These questions annoyed me. So did the Christian workers. Why were they so interested in me? Today, I'm grateful. They caused me to face those questions and make the right choices.

I recall a buddy from my early 20s. He was tough, hard-talking, heavy drinking, two-fisted. Then, all of a sudden, he came to me and apologized for some criticisms he had made about me.

Man . . . this I couldn't understand. He further puzzled me by turning down cigarettes. When it came time to share the drinks, he said "No, thanks."

When we called his house, his mother said:

"He's not here. He went to prayer meeting." Or some other strange place.

He even went to a store and paid them back for some tools he had once stolen. Why all this?

He explained that one night, out of boredom, he walked into a church and listened to the speaker describe what sin is. That clobbered him so much that he found himself walking forward when the speaker invited people to do that in order to receive Christ.

Of course, we thought it would blow over.

But it didn't.

He became one of the gentlest, most selfless people I have ever known. And that was at least forty years ago.

144

A sermon launched him on that road, and the other resources of the church have kept him on that road. His example is one of the reasons I am on that same path.

UP WITH MINISTERS!

When people are critical of ministers, I ask:
"Which minister? Which one?"

Granted, if you would rank all the ministers you know (that's probably not many), they would rank from the best to the worst. That's true also of psychiatrists, physicians, dentists, lawyers, CPA's, etc.

I have specialized also in counseling ministers. They are the finest single group of people I know anything about. When a minister falls into difficulty, it's because he quit following his own instructions — like anyone else. I've seen ministers (even some who have helped me) suddenly forsake their own advice. Too bad. It was good advice.

Ministers are the custodians of the most important information in the world — the contents of the Bible.

UP WITH CHURCHES!

I hear people criticize someone who is excited about his church. What's wrong with that? You ought to be excited about your church. You should enthusiastically want other people in your church so they can share the help you're receiving.

There are many kinds of churches. In my church, the ideal during the worship period is quietness. You can hear a pin drop. But I've been in others where everyone is talking at once. There are many styles. They won't all suit you, but they will suit someone.

When someone is critical of "churches," again I ask them:

"Which church?"

Then I remind them that churches can rank from the best to the worst . . . as do schools, universities, hospitals, businesses, football teams, any group of institutions.

According to my observations you can get some of the best help possible as a person, marriage partner, or parent from the church, church-related groups, and their personnel.

TEN WAYS THE CHURCH HELPS

Let me point out some of the aids available through these groups.

The sermon. There is no better help for you than weekly exposure to biblical principles. Many sermons are dry to listen to. So are many vital university lectures.

We need information as well as inspiration. Through sermons, multitudes have found God, the inner resources He provides, His instruction and guidance.

The Sunday school. Keep your eyes open in the Sunday school and you can observe the gamut of life — from the cradle to the grave. Few places give you this opportunity. You'll see saints and hypocrites. You can see what happens to people who accept biblical teachings and what happens to those who reject them.

The Sunday school lets you listen to the teachings of laymen or allows you to do some teaching yourself. You can raise questions and exchange views. Find new friends. If you have a knack for administration, your talent might help make the Sunday school run smoother.

Men's, Women's, or Youth Groups. You can join specialized groups. Some are organized around sports. Others help handicapped people like the blind, deaf, crippled.

There are groups for the retired, for calling on people in the name of the church, for discussion and education.

You can make friendships, help one another, observe what happens when biblical principles are obeyed or disobeyed. Specialized groups give you a chance to use your talent and training.

Boards, committees. Obviously, someone makes policy decisions, applies good business management principles and methods to operate churches and church-related organizations. You can share your expertise in these areas.

Music. The medium of music helps us worship God. This is a double-barreled thing. Music in worship inspires us and helps us establish principles in our minds — in addition to the preaching and teaching — through the act of enjoying the music and listening to the words.

The other side of the coin is that music gives people a chance to serve through their musical talents.

Consultations. The church is a great resource center. You can exchange information with people you respect (be they laymen or professional staff) in such areas as marriage, family, finances, education, recreation. You may help others who need help in these areas.

The range of advice is limited only by the expertise of the staff and fellow church members.

Bible studies. You can enjoy the experience and knowledge of professionals and laymen, in and out of the church. You will find people in the church who specialize in Bible studies and in a variety of areas. They help increase your biblical knowledge and how to apply what you learn.

Again, if you have expertise of your own, you might do some teaching yourself.

Fellowship. You're not alone. I've traveled all over the world by plane, car, jeep, oxcart, and dugout canoe, and walked mountain trails and jungle paths. Wherever you go, you can find fellow Christians. You will help yourself by seeking them out.

You can meet Christians in your profession, your job, or in areas of special interest. There is a bond that binds — on all levels.

Conferences. In a person's profession, you constantly go to seminars to learn more about how to better perform your job.

The church, likewise, has many excellent seminars and conferences on many subjects.

You can meet people from other churches and other groups. For a day, a weekend, a week, you can leave your daily routine behind and focus on the Bible and related subjects.

Camps. Here your children can have intimate contact with other children and receive some concentrated instruction from counselors, speakers, and teachers. Adults and families can combine a vacation with instruction, inspiration, and Christian fellowship.

An amazing number of people have had their lives turned around at a Christian camp.

UP WITH DENOMINATIONS!

Then there are the denominations. I say "Hooray!" for them. They make camps available. Youth programs. Helpful organizations for other age groups. Materials. Books. Magazines. Speakers. Other personnel.

You couldn't do it without denominations.

Granted, you can rank denominations just as you do Christians, ministers, and churches.

UP WITH SPECIALIZED ORGANIZATIONS!

There are groups that specialize. We mentioned many of them earlier. There are also the publishing companies . . . Child Evangelism . . . Christian Service Brigade . . . Pioneer Girls . . . Awana . . . many others. They serve people from all churches and denominations. We urge you to use their services.

These agencies are an aid to the church.

WHO GOES TO HOSPITALS?

You can liken the church and related groups to a hospital. You expect to find sick people there. They are in varying stages of health. Some were there before. They recovered. But they didn't take care of themselves and got sick again. The hospital admits them again and again. Doctors, nurses, and related personnel help them each time.

In the church, people are in varying stages of sinfulness. Some recover rapidly and fall again. Some just pretend to be interested.

They leave the church, neglect God's teachings, then come limping back in. The church personnel and its members are there to help once more. Others grow steadily and apply biblical principles to their lives on a daily basis.

YOUR CHOICE . . .

Why are you there?

Will you reject the teachings because other people do? Hardly.

If you reject the biblical teachings you hear week after week in the church, you do so because you want to, not because someone else does. If you *want to* accept Christ, no one can stop you. If you *want to* let God bathe your heart with His love, no one can stop you.

If you want to cooperate with your partner, no one can stop you. If you want to make a lifetime commitment to your partner, no one can stop you.

Because you love your partner and submit yourself to the marriage does not mean your partner will do so. This is a personal matter each partner must face alone, and before God. But no one can stop you from making up your mind.

The choice is yours.

13 / A Baker's Dozen . . . for Married Couples

13 / A Baker's Dozen . . . for Married Couples

I'VE HEARD THAT ONE BEFORE!

That's what you'll be saying as you read this chapter, for it's time to look back at the last twelve chapters and remind yourself of the principles in this book. As you reconsider these principles consider them as more than just words — consider them as thirteen (a "baker's dozen") friends who can help make your marriage better.

WITH A LITTLE HELP . . . FROM THIRTEEN FRIENDS

1. *Most marriages begin with a strong, magnetic attraction for each other.*

> The LORD God said, "It is not good for the man to be alone; I will make him a helper suitable for him" (Gen. 2:18).

God put a drive in us that irresistibly draws a woman and a man together. You naturally team up.

Remember those dating days? Suddenly, to be near your boyfriend or girl friend was the most satisfying privilege in the world.

Marriage was the healthy result.

> For this cause [she is suitable for him] a man shall leave his father and his mother, and shall cleave to his wife; and they shall become one flesh (Gen. 2:24).

2. *However, marriage unmasks what the Bible de-*

scribes as "self-seeking" and "deeds of the flesh."

Self-seeking.

> All of us like sheep have gone astray, each of us has turned to his own way; but the LORD has caused the iniquity of us all to fall on Him (Isa. 53:6).

The "iniquity" mentioned in this verse is *turning to your own way*. In a word: self-seeking. Marriage magnifies self-seeking instead of eliminating it.

Deeds of the flesh. Marriage magnifies the deeds of the flesh. The Bible describes them as:

> . . . immorality, impurity, sensuality, idolatry, sorcery, enmities, strife, jealousy, outbursts of anger, disputes, dissensions, factions, envyings, drunkenness, carousings, and things like these, of which I forewarn you just as I have forewarned you that those who practice such things shall not inherit the kingdom of God (Gal. 5:19-21).

You expect marriage to make you loving, kind, and unselfish.

But . . . no.

Instead, it reveals self-seeking and deeds of the flesh.

3. *Deadlocks develop when opinions differ.* Your reactions to these clashes (self-seeking and deeds of the flesh) erect an invisible wall, which is built one brick (incident) at a time.

This wall short-circuits tenderness, fellowship, and the will to make the partnership grow.

It happens to newlyweds, the educated, the wealthy, the healthy, old-timers, the uneducated, the sick, and the poor.

But this wall can be dismantled.

4. *You need help from an outside source, God Himself, through Jesus Christ.* Help comes from God, and neither people nor circumstances can interfere.

But you are separated from God.

Why?

> Your iniquities [self-seeking] have made a separation between you and your God, and your sins (deeds of the flesh) have hid His face from you, so that He does not hear (Isa. 59:2).

How can you bridge the gap? By asking Jesus Christ to come into your life.

> But as many as received Him [Jesus], to them He gave the right to become children of God, even to those who believe in His name (John 1:12).

Without taking this step, there is no way to remove the wall between you and your partner.

Once you take this step, you are a child of God and can claim the resources that only God can make available.

5. *The oil that eliminates friction is God's love.*

> The love of God has been poured out within our hearts through the Holy Spirit who was given to us (Rom. 5:5).

Like oil, God's love has many different elements, First Corinthians 13:4-8 says that God's love:

> . . . is patient . . . is kind . . . is not jealous . . . is not arrogant . . . does not seek its own, is not provoked, does not take into account a wrong suffered, does not rejoice in unrighteousness, but rejoices with the truth; bears all things, believes all things, hopes all things, endures all things . . . never fails.

God's love makes a gentleman or a lady out of you. These elements of His love will restore the thrill of hugging and kissing, the warmth of friendship.

With His love as a resource, you can face the problems, get rid of the friction, and find a way to resolve your differences.

6. *Marriage is a partnership.* A husband-wife team work together to design a harness both can wear.

> Make my joy complete by being of the same mind, maintaining the same love, united in spirit, intent on one purpose. Do nothing from selfishness or empty conceit, but with humility of mind let each regard one another as more important than himself (Phil. 2:2,3).

It's like doubles in tennis. Partners cooperate instead of compete. Husband and wife are teammates, not opponents, as they dedicate themselves to seek a meeting of minds.

Where do you begin to come to a meeting of minds?

7. You start by accepting the need for leadership. In other words, who will be the boss?

Why do two married people who have the love of God in their hearts need a leader? Because, when a decision must be made, however small, and opinions differ, there is no other way to settle the differences.

Leadership involves three characteristics. They are: *cooperation, submission,* and *commitment.* We call them *the big three.*

They provide the basis for defining the guidelines and rules for making your marriage better. They are the foundation of a good family plan.

8. Cooperation — the first key. Husband and wife decide to dedicate time and effort in developing a mutually agreeable way of life.

> . . . be subject to one another in the fear of Christ (Eph. 5:21).

Cooperation depends on a family plan. Regular formal or informal conferences between husband and wife are held to assign responsibilities and develop policies, procedures, and rules both can live with.

These meetings can be held in the car, the kitchen, the living room, the bedroom — anywhere.

Two attitudes pervade these meetings: (1) each partner means to serve the other, and (2) both will be bound by the decisions made by the partnership. Daily effort, constant examination, and frequent changes keep your plan going.

9. Submission — the second key. Someone must have the last word. Any two or more people who must cooperate, no matter how friendly or dedicated, will ultimately become deadlocked. Someone must break that deadlock.

In marriage, it's the husband.

> Wives, be subject to your own husbands, as to the Lord (Eph. 5:22).

The husband settles an unresolved deadlock. The wife should participate vigorously and forthrightly in the search for mutually agreeable decisions.

The husband should think twice, or more, before

going against his wife's judgment. If the wife still disagrees with a husband's tie-breaking decision, she should say so. The husband has two options when there is a deadlock:

1. Make the decision himself.
2. Ask his wife to make it.

Once done, both husband and wife submit to the decision and do all in their power to make it work.

10. *Commitment — the third key. A husband's number one priority is to serve his wife.* He should love his wife as he loves himself and submit to the responsibility for maintaining a wholesome relationship to her. This relationship to his wife takes priority over work, church, recreation, even the children.

A family seldom breaks up if the husband truly loves his wife (with God's love) and is committed unto death to make the marriage work.

11. *A good marriage effectively handles the daily routines.* Learning how to properly handle daily routines is an art a husband and wife don't master overnight.

Blending routines requires continuous study, trial and error, give and take. It involves many friendly meetings. Only the love of God in both partners will make harmonious decisions possible.

12. *The three most common trouble spots in marriage are sex, money, and sudden changes.*

Sexual problems. When you do not respond to one another sexually, look elsewhere for the answer. There will be a wall of deadlocks and hostility dividing you. Remove the wall, and you will restore sexual harmony.

There is a specific directive in the Bible to guide you in your physical relationships:

> Let the husband fulfill his duty to his wife, and likewise also the wife to her husband. The wife does not have authority over her own body, but the husband does; and likewise also the husband does not have authority over his own body, but the wife does. Stop depriving one another, except by agreement for a time that you may devote yourselves to prayer, and come together again lest Satan tempt you because of your lack of self-control (1 Cor. 7:3-5).

Take this "commandment" seriously and you will

see that the basic issues are submission to one another, and maintaining a healthy spiritual life.

There is a warning here. If you deprive one another, you can expect your partner to be subject to serious temptation.

Money problems can split a marriage. The following principles can help you prevent such a disaster:

1. Spend less than you earn.
2. Face your creditors. If you're in trouble, ask for their help and counsel.
3. A competent financial advisor can help greatly.
4. Allow a certain percentage of every paycheck for savings, risk money, and a tithe to God.
5. Make sure you have a mutually agreeable plan for managing your money.

Sudden changes. Look on them as a way to grow. How well you meet the sudden changes of life depends on how committed you are to God and to your partner.

You can count on sudden changes. But they are for the best, no matter how bad they seem.

> And we know that God causes all things to work together for good to those who love God, and to those who are called according to His purpose (Rom. 8:28).

Maybe the sudden change is hard to understand. How can this circumstance work together for good? For a child of God, with His love in your heart, it all adds up to good. As the Bible says:

> Rejoice always; pray without ceasing; in everything give thanks; for this is God's will for you in Christ Jesus (1 Thess. 5:16-18).

13. *Let the church and church-related groups help strengthen your marriage.* There are four ways:

1. Inspiration
2. Instruction
3. Fellowship
4. Service (participation)

Through church and related agencies, you get weekly exposure to biblical principles. You can observe (and learn from watching) the gamut of life in the church, where you can see what happens to people who accept biblical teachings — and what happens to those who reject them.

We have an opportunity to "take in," to grow as persons, as well as many opportunities to develop our talents through service.

YOUR MARRIAGE CAN BE BETTER

There they are: thirteen steps from friction to fellowship in marriage. Memorize them. Practice them.

Then, as a child of God, you can have a new zest for life.

Bring on the future!
And a better marriage!